WHAT ARE PEOPLE SAYING ABOUT THIS BOOK?

Solo Dei Gloria

I have known Russ (then "Rusty") Nebhut since he was a student in my Greek class at Dallas Christian College quite some years ago. Even then, I remember his enthusiasm for two things: Biblical studies and pastoral ministry. He was an excellent student, in part because he found Scripture and all its associated disciplines fascinating, but even more, because he wanted to apply Scripture in ministry to people.

This book is the fruit of those two passions in his life. You will find in it a careful, in-depth exploration of Scripture, coupled with profound application to the relationship every Christian can have with the Father – indeed, should have, if, as Russ presents, we simply better understood what the Scripture teaches about the Father's heart for His people.

I appreciate the teaching in this book, but most especially how Russ applies that teaching to many common misconceptions people have about foundational issues of who God is, who man is, and what it means to be saved – even Christians with many years in the faith.

Thank you, Russ, for your ministry, your heart, this book, and the privilege of reviewing it.

John Schirle
Professor Emeritus Dallas Christian College

I have known Russell Nebhut for many years. He and his wife babysat for our children who are now nearly fifty years old. Russ was one of my students at Dallas Christian. I have always had great respect for him.

His book shows us that God created all that exists for us to have relationship with Him. He is a "trinity" and so are we. He is Father, Son, Spirit; we are body, soul, spirit. When we follow his Son, His Spirit lives in union with our spirit; they both witness together that we are children of God. (Romans 8:16) We can know God intimately by this spiritual communion. Sin separated us from God and made relationship with him impossible. But the death of Jesus on the cross, followed by his resurrection, made it possible to have this relationship restored.

It is exciting for me to remember that Russ was a serious student of the word—and that he still is. His passion and deep desire has always been to study and learn the scriptures to know God better. He has continued to grow through the years, and I am proud to call him my past student and my friend.

May God bless you, Russ. And may this book be a blessing to many.

Dr. Mark Berrier

Russ Nebhut

REVEALED GOD

Reclaiming the Lost Image of God
and the Power of True Relationship

www.Emerge.pub

REVEALED GOD: Reclaiming the Lost Image of God and the Power of True Relationship

Copyright ©2022 Russ Nebhut

All Rights Reserved. Except as permitted under the U.S. Copyright Act of 1976, no part of this publication may be reproduced, distributed, or transmitted in any form by any means, or stored in a database or retrieval system, without the prior written permission of the author and/or publisher.

Scriptures marked ESV are taken from the THE HOLY BIBLE, ENGLISH STANDARD VERSION (ESV): Scriptures taken from THE HOLY BIBLE, ENGLISH STANDARD VERSION ® Copyright© 2001 by Crossway, a publishing ministry of Good News Publishers. Used by permission.

Published by:
Emerge Publishing, LLC
9521 B Riverside Parkway, Suite 243
Tulsa, OK 74137
www.emerge.pub

Library of Congress Cataloging-in-Publication Data:

ISBN: 978-1-954966-26-0   Paperback
E-book available exclusively on Kindle

BISAC:
REL012120   **RELIGION** / Christian Living / Spiritual Growth
REL012070   **RELIGION** / Christian Living / Personal Growth

Printed in the United States
rev. 1-5-23

CONTENTS

What are People Saying about This Book? 1

Foreword 9

Acknowledgments by the Author 13

Introduction 15

Chapter 1 Created In The Image of God 27

          Examine the Account of Creation Revealed
in Genesis Chapter 1 33

          What Does it Mean to be Given Dominion 34

Chapter 2 Humans are Created

          As Trinitarian Beings Body – Soul – Spirit 39

          The Words for Body 42

          The Words for Soul 48

          The Words for Spirit 52

Chapter 3 The Human Spirit is Created by God 57

Chapter 4 Life with God Before and After the Fall into Sin 64

	Adam's Relationship with God Before the Fall 64
	Adam's Relationship with God After the Fall 70
	The Existence of Man Apart from God 71
	False Religions - Why do They Seem to Satisfy? 72
	They Make Sense to Human Beings 73
	Larger than Man, but Man can Comprehend Them. 73
	The Human Spirit Seeks to Reclaim what was Lost by its Own Actions - Works Appeal. 74
	The Illusion of Progress 75
	Here are Several Scripture Passages in which God Reveals the Appeals of False Beliefs: 77
	Why Man's Search for the "Spiritual" can Never Give Reconciliation or Peace 79
	God is Incomprehensible 81
Chapter 5	What Happens at Conversion 84
Chapter 6	How do We Live in Our New Relationship With God as One Who is Re-Born? 92
	Created in the Image of God 96
Chapter 7	To be a Chosen People 104
	The Covenant with Israel 111
	The Covenant with Abraham 114
	Return to Mt. Sinai and the Covenant with Israel ... 116

Chapter 8	Creation of Man and Woman Opposites but Complete in Each Other	120
	Human Beings were Created to Live in Fellowship with One Another and with God	123
Chapter 9	Fellowship with God	130
	The Promise is Given with a Visible Act of God	133
	Jesus is the Action of God for Us	134
Chapter 10	The Heart of God Yearns for His Children	140
	It can be Difficult for Us to Believe In God's Limitless Love	144
Chapter 11	What the Church on Earth Should be	148
	The Two Ways of Jesus	157
	What is God's Desire for His People?	161
Chapter 12	God Knows All About You and He Still Loves You and Wants You	163
Chapter 13	Our Future Life with God – A Vision of Imagination	168
	To Fully Know and to be Fully Known	170
	Glorifying God in Eternity	173
Epilogue		177

FOREWORD

In a youth camp near wind turbines in the scrub trees of West Texas near I-20, two men gathered for a few days to do a deep-dive study of what it means to be 'made in God's image.' School was in session, so there were no campers, and we had the place to ourselves. We gathered our best resources, original language texts, study software, and sleeping bags, and settled in for a few days. We had a theological 'itch' we had to scratch - are we two-part or three-part 'images' of God? Is the spirit equal to the soul, as some say, or are they distinct in Scripture? How much overlap is there in use? Those questions were the genesis of this book, and our time together in study is one of my favorite memories.

I met Russ a few years before this when he was installed at a sister (really 'daughter') congregation two towns over from the place where I was serving. Our years at seminary overlapped, but we really did not know each other there. We connected with each other because of the Spirit's work to place us in neighboring congregations, even though we were from different parts of the country - he from Texas and I from Ohio. And despite the fact that I was a decade older, we found a fellowship through the Holy Spirit and the joy of serving others with the Gospel. Plus, we played a little golf at the local 9-hole course a few times a month and enjoyed the competition with each other. And truth be told, we also supported each other in the tough times that marriage and ministry bring to daily life. We are still sinners, and we still call each other to account! I knew he was having a tough day when he would call me more than once a day. I always listened. My friend needed my ear. We respected each other - he respected my age and experience (I am a second-career pastor), and I respected his scholarship. We became life-long friends in the sense of this passage:

> *A man of many companions may come to ruin,*
> *but there is a friend who sticks closer than a brother.*
>
> Proverbs 18:24 ESV

When Russ proposed this short study session, I was happy to come along, even though I wondered why. He is much more a Biblical scholar than I. My specialties are Systematics and Biblical Counseling. However, the time we spent with God's Word was enlightening. I think it improved both of us in terms of our understanding of God and how He thinks of His children. I know that for my ministry, it has come out in how I counsel and teach and care for my wife. We found a deeper layer to life as we explored and learned from the Scriptures. Our approach was to leave our preconceived thoughts behind and let the texts speak to us. And speak they did.

Those thoughts have percolated in both our minds over the many years since that session. Russ, being the quality teacher he is, also wanted to capture what we learned, and he has further developed it in a lasting form like a book, in such a way that you, the reader, can take a bit of our study session into your mind and heart with the help of the Holy Spirit and find the incredible richness of 'being made in God's image' too. To Him be all the glory!

Joe Ardy

ACKNOWLEDGMENTS BY THE AUTHOR

I would like to begin by saying thank you for selecting this book. It is a book rich in the thoughts and the heart of one single man who has yearned to know the heart of God.

Over the years, I have discovered a depth of love for God, which has only been made possible because of God's Limitless Love for me. This book has been a journey of almost ten years in both research and the tangible experience of living as a child of God in the midst of the brokenness of this world.

As you probably know, life is a journey best taken with friends. Those closest to me have been patiently supportive along every step of this incredible process of God revealing His truth in the wisdom of His Word, alongside countless affirmations seen in the hearts and lives of His children. I want to express my appreciation to my wife, Stephanie, for her devotion and love for me. We shared countless discussions during the process of writing this book, and her wisdom and insights have helped me immensely. In addition to this, my friend and brother in the faith, Rev. Joseph Ardy, was instrumental in the study and understanding of the distinction between the body, soul, and spirit of a human being. The retreat we shared together, taking time for research on this subject, is what spurred the original thought of what is now the book you hold in your hand. Beyond these two people who have blessed my life in such great ways, I would be remiss if I did not simply say that countless men and women have written about the love of God in the past. Many have sought to write and share the truths they have discovered. I am indebted to their wisdom and the working of God in their lives. We stand on the shoulders of all the great saints of God who have gone before us.

My prayer is that as you read *Revealed God*, you will begin your own journey into discovering the limitless love of God, which fills His heart for you. I encourage you to plumb the depths of what you have experienced in your own life and what our Father has revealed in His Word and through the wisdom of others. May you be blessed as your Father reveals to you, in an intimate and personal way, who you are in His eyes and how His love holds you in the depths of His heart.

INTRODUCTION

A life of intimacy with God is characterized by joy.

– Oswald Chambers

It is hard for any of us to imagine what eternity is truly like. Each of us has an idea in our mind's eye of what it will be like when we are welcomed into the kingdom of heaven. But as we begin our journey together, I want to challenge you to think for a moment of eternity. Think of eternity when nothing in all creation existed – only God!

This book is not a theological dissertation on the nature of God. I will make some assumptions concerning a basic understanding of what the Word of God reveals concerning Who God is and how He has revealed Himself.

God is Trinity! Three persons, yet one God as is revealed in Scripture and confessed both in the Christian creeds and throughout Church history. The Father, Son, and Holy Spirit live in perfect unity and harmony. The Father loves the Son and the Spirit. The Son loves the Father and the Spirit. The Spirit loves the Father and the Son. A perfect relationship of love.

Introduction

It has often been asked, *"Since God knew man would sin, why did He create the world, to begin with?"* The answer is found in the nature of God Himself. God is love! The apostle John writes, *"Anyone who does not love does not know God, because God is love"* 1 John 4:8. Love is a unique noun in Scripture. Love is often described as an emotion, but in reality, it is much more.

When John writes the above passage, he uses the term "agape." It is one of four types of love that is revealed in ancient writings, three of which are found in Scripture. The one type of love which is not seen in the Bible is the word "storge." Storge is described by the ancient writers as the love a wolf has for her pups. It is an instinctive love that moves the wolf to care for her pups, feeding and protecting them until they are grown. Then, they are kicked out of the den. This love is found in nature and not among people.

Of the three types of love seen throughout the Word of God, "eros" is probably the easiest to understand. The word eros is the root of the English word "erotic." Erotic love is a blessing from God! It is a very passionate and emotional love that is perfectly expressed between a husband and wife as they share the intimacy of the marriage bed. A husband is to have an erotic desire for his wife and the wife for her husband. Yet, when perverted because of man's sinful nature, eros becomes what God never intended it to be. It is this powerful, physical love that causes a husband's roaming eye. The lack of eros in a marriage leaves a wife susceptible to the advances of a man other than her husband. Eros is very much in charge when a young couple is pregnant outside of marriage. Eros is what drives the pornography industry and is at the root of all sexual sins.

"Philos" is a true and powerful love of friendship and relationship. It is exemplified in the relationship between young David and Jonathan. These two men had a love relationship with each other. Many have used this relationship as an example of homosexuality in the Old Testament. Nothing could be further from the truth. These two men, who were not related, became so close in their relationship with each other that their love for each other was stronger than the love of father and son or of brother to brother. "Philos" is a real self-sacrificing love that two people have for each other. It is a love that would move one friend to die for another, if necessary. "Philos" falls short in that it is unable to love all people equally. It is a very special love, but not the love that God has for all mankind. "Eros" and "Philos" describe the love which is shared between people. Each has its blessed use, and each has been corrupted by the fall into sin, and as such, each can be perverted.

When the Scripture speaks of the love God has for all people, the term used is "agape." "Agape" has a facet of "eros" in that it is strongly emotional. The true nature of love found in "Philos" is found in agape because this love would truly move a person to die for the person who is loved. But unlike the other two types of love, agape is a pure love that loves because it can and because it chooses to love. Agape loves everyone equally, even those who would not accept this love or reject it. It is this type of love that God has for all people. A love filled with emotion! A love that desires an intimate relationship! A love that is willing to sacrifice everything for the one who is loved!

The uniqueness of agape is that it has its origin in God, extends from Him to us, and through us to touch the lives of others. It is again the apostle John who aids us in our understanding; *"In this is love, not that we have loved God but that he loved us and sent his Son to be the propitiation for our sins"* 1 John 4:10. This text reveals God's love for us in that Jesus came as the One who would make the payment for sin, "propitiation" or more correctly stated in the ancient text, Jesus became the "sin offering" or the "atoning sacrifice" for us.

When humanity was alienated from God because of sin, and when we, in truth, did not want God or His love, He loved us. We were enemies of God who were loved by Him and saved by Him because He loved us with true agape. It is a self-sacrificing love that loves all equally! Love which moved Him to hang on a cross for all people.

I lay all this foundation to aid you in your thoughts of eternity. Eternity, before creation existed, was filled with our God of love, Who shared His life in the blessed Trinitarian union. God existed in Himself, and all was perfect. Filled with agape, God made a choice to create. Because He knows the future, God could see the day Adam and Eve would fall into sin. He saw the corruption of His perfect creation and the agony of creation itself groaning under the burden of sin.

> *"For the creation was subjected to futility, not willingly, but because of him who subjected it, in hope that the creation itself will be set free from its bondage to decay and obtain the freedom of the glory of the children of God. For we know that the whole creation has been groaning together in the pains of childbirth until now"* (Romans 8:20-22).

It would have been better for God if He had allowed creation to be a passing thought. It was His agape that would not allow this to happen! Moved by agape, God created because He chose to love all people, even before He created us. Love which moved Him to love you even before He created you. A love that moved Him to choose to create you even knowing He would one day have to die for you.

One of the greatest joys in the life of a pastor is to have a young couple stand before him and pledge their love for each other before God, seeking His blessings as they begin their married life together. There are very few instances where a couple who are married is satisfied simply being a couple for the rest of their lives. As the months and years pass, the love they have for each other grows and deepens. Because of this, as time passes, there is a desire on the part of a young couple to bring a child into this world. In many aspects, the child becomes the focus of their love! Extending from their love for each other and born of their bodies, a new life is created. The love present in their lives together wants to give more. The two become three, and their love is expanded, and all are blessed.

Now think of eternity! God, in harmony and unity, exists forever and lacks nothing. The heart of God did not need anything, but God wanted something more. His desire was to create so He could love. God wanted an object, a focus of His love. He wanted to create people so He could love us and bless us.

There was a time in history when it was believed the world was flat! Later, man believed the earth was the center of the universe. Today we know we are only one small planet in the midst of endless space. While not wanting to turn back the hands of time, it may serve to illustrate my point by once again placing the earth at the center of the universe.

All of creation exists and is sustained each moment because this world is the object of God's desire and love. God created the galaxies with millions of stars to give us wonder, but all of it was created because of this solar system, as the third planet circling the sun was His heart's desire. Everything in all creation exists because God created this place, earth, for a purpose. He created a perfect world to be a place of blessing for the people He chose to create. The desire of God's heart was to create people to love. Agape moved Him to create, even knowing those He created would cause Him pain. It is the same for a young couple who is blessed with a child. They know the future will have nights of illness and patching up scraped knees.

There will be times when the child will disobey and disappoint, but this does not deter a young couple. There is so much love they can't help but share it with the child. There is so much love (agape) in God He could not help but share it. He created us so He could love us. He continues to sustain all creation so He can love. The only reason creation still exists is that God still wants to love the people He created.

From eternity the heart of God yearned to express His love and to have us as the object of His love. From eternity God spoke, and creation came into being. Everything centered on that sixth day when He would fulfill the reason that everything was made. God formed man from the dust of the ground and shared His life, and man became a living being. The account in Genesis states after each day of creation that it was "good" (Genesis 1). Following the creation of the man and the woman on the sixth day of creation, God declared that it was "very good" (Genesis 1:31). Bear with me for a moment, if you will. Genesis chapter 1 reveals the six days of creation and all that God did when He brought creation into existence by the power of His Word. There have been many people confused by the account being partially repeated in Genesis chapter two. While chapter one gives us a quick overview, chapter two reveals in detail the creation of the man and the woman, which was the purpose of all the rest of creation.

God is a relational being! The Father, Son, and Holy Spirit live in a relationship of love with one another. As creation was formed, each step of the way, it was declared by God to be good. It was not until man and woman were created that it was said to be "very good." This is because while all creation was good, it was not yet perfect until the woman was created. Genesis chapter two says, *"Then the LORD God said, "It is not good for the man to be alone; I will make him a helper suitable for him"* Genesis 2:18. There was something lacking that needed to be completed before God could declare all of creation to be "very good." Creation was perfect or complete when the man and woman were both created and were thus enabled to live in a relationship with one another. Both man and woman were created in God's image, meaning they were created as relational beings. God does not live in isolation, and we were never created to live alone. As those who bear His image, we were created to live in a relationship with Him and with each other. The unique relationship between a man and woman (husband and wife) reveals the intimate uniqueness of the image of God in the world.

The man was alone in the garden. God had created man in His own image, and this meant God had created in the heart of man the ability to love as He loved. For the man to be able to love as God loves, he would need someone to focus his love upon. It was God's love for the man and His desire to allow the man to share love that moved God to create the woman. Man was created to be the object of God's love. The woman was created so man could fulfill the image of God and love as God loves. Together the man and woman were complete and blessed. They were loved and able to love.

Introduction

In this world of perfection and love, God enjoyed fellowship with the man and woman. We do not know exactly how long Adam and Eve lived in the garden before they fell into sin and were expelled from their home. What we do know is this time in the garden was truly a blissful life in the truest sense of the word. The passage of Scripture that immediately follows the fall into sin gives us some insight into their life in the garden. *"And they heard the sound of the LORD God walking in the garden in the cool of the day, and the man and his wife hid themselves from the presence of the LORD God among the trees of the garden"* Genesis 3:8.

Adam and Eve were not scared of the fact that God had come into the garden, as if it was the first time He had done this. The verse reads that it was not unusual for God to come into the garden, but this time they hid themselves. The cool of the day is a time when all creation settles down for the evening. As the sun begins to set late in the day, the birds return to their nests, the does bed down with their fawns, and all creation is tucked in for the night. Like a father entering a child's room for a good night hug and a bedtime story, God enters the garden to walk with the ones He loves. The image of God walking with the man and woman is an image of intimacy and love. The image given for our mind's eye to see is of God entering the garden each evening and walking arm in arm with Adam and Eve. He would listen as they told Him of their experiences of the day and what they had seen and learned. He would bless them, and they would marvel in His love. This was exactly what God had desired, what agape had moved Him to do. The unusual event in this passage is that Adam and Eve hid themselves from God this time. The passage seems to imply that each evening Adam and Eve would run to meet God when He entered the garden, but this time they ran the other way. Sin had entered into God's children, and as a result, they would be different, and all creation would be different.

How many times have we seen or experienced in our own lives this agape for a child who has fully and totally disappointed us? How many parents have spent hundreds, even thousands of dollars, to get their child out of trouble? Some parents will do this over and over again, hoping someday their child will learn to make different choices. Is there any limit to the love a parent is able to have for a child? Now, turn your attention to the heart of God. Is there any limit to the love God has for His children? How many times have we, all people, messed up what the Bible calls sin? Is there a limit to His love? Is there a line we can finally cross over where God will say, *"That's it! I have had it. No more! I will no longer love you."* The answer is a resounding "No!" There is no limit to the love God has for all people or the sacrifice He would make to love us! No limit to the price He would pay to have us as His own once more and be able to share His love with us.

The remainder of this book will explore the depths of God's love. The marvel of creation and the beauty and power of a God who loves each of us with unfailing love, a love which captivates the heart of God and, if we let it, will fill our lives, and change us for all eternity.

CHAPTER ONE

CREATED IN THE IMAGE OF GOD

Then God said, "Let us make man in our image, after our likeness. And let them have dominion over the fish of the sea and over the birds of the heavens and over the livestock and over all the earth and over every creeping thing that creeps on the earth."

– Genesis 1:26

What exactly is the image of God? There have been many answers over the centuries and, in fact, throughout human history, which have sought to explore the image of God. Some have totally missed the mark, and some have come close. Most, if not all, have never dared to go deep enough to explore the depths of what God is truly like and the image in which mankind was created.

Within the current focus of Christianity, the idea of exploring the nature of God and how this applies to humanity has made a transition from where it was centuries ago to what it has become today, very shallow and filled with formula statements about God that carry very little meaning. For example, we say God is "holy" or "just" without ever exploring what this truly means. God is Trinity, but we never seek to understand what it actually means that God is three in One and One in three. While it is beyond our grasp to fully understand the mystery of the Trinity, we should not stop with the simple examples we use to teach this truth to our children. There is much more we can understand if we simply listen to what God has revealed about Himself in scripture.

What was God like in eternity prior to creation? We have this image of God the Father as some distant, unyielding, stalwart figure who is uncaring and harsh. This, of course, stands in stark contrast to John 3:16, *"For God so loved the world."* How can God the Father be uncaring and at the same time love us enough to send Jesus to be our Savior? How is it possible for a God of love to be unconcerned about the struggles you face in your life, be it trouble at work or the kids misbehaving? In truth, God is intimately concerned about you and everything happening in your life at every moment. To understand this, we need to move away from the current views of God and discover anew what God is truly like.

It has been said that there is a God-shaped hole in the heart of every human being. The seventeenth-century scientist and theologian Blaise Pascal wrote of this after what seemed to be a dramatic conversion experience. Pascal writes: *"There is a God-shaped vacuum in the heart of each man which cannot be satisfied by any created thing but only by God the Creator, made know through Jesus Christ."* History seems to bear out the reality of this. Every culture throughout history has sought God in one way or another. From the ancient world right up to modern day, one truth is evident, in the absence of understanding what God is truly like, people create a god in their own image.

If humanity were still perfect and holy as it was at first, the image of God, which was ingrained in the heart of man, would be similar to who God truly is. However, because of sin and the corruption it brings, a god is created, which is very much corrupted, as we are. From the ancient gods of Asherah and Moleck to the Greek gods of Zeus and Hera to the Norse gods of Odin and Thor, all the gods of the ancient world simply displayed the character of man with heightened powers. In each and every case, the gods of man's imagination were self-centered and selfish, embodying all the greed and prideful desires which are the focus of all human attention.

Being then God's offspring, we ought not to think that the divine being is like gold Being then God's offspring, we ought not to think that the divine being is like gold or silver or stone, an image formed by the art and imagination of man. Acts 17:29

> *For his invisible attributes, namely, his eternal power and divine nature, have been clearly perceived, ever since the creation of the world, in the things that have been made. So they are without excuse. For although they knew God, they did not honor him as God or give thanks to him, but they became futile in their thinking, and their foolish hearts were darkened. Claiming to be wise, they became fools, and exchanged the glory of the immortal God for images resembling mortal man and birds and animals and creeping things.* Romans 1:20-23

History has demonstrated that in the absence of an understanding of who God truly is and what He is like, we have created gods who encapsulate all the worst in humanity. The reasons for this are no doubt varied but suffice to say that this understanding of who God is lets man off the hook. If our god is like we are, then we can't be all that bad! We are justified in seeking to gain an advantage over others. We are simply that kind of god when we lie, cheat, steal, or kill. There is no true accountability and, therefore, no true responsibility. The challenge we face is to seek to understand who God truly is and what He is actually like, and in this, to discover what is in His heart concerning each of us!

So, what is the image of God? Is God holy? Is God just? Is God concerned with this world, or are we simply on our own here and left to face judgment in the end? The nature of God is tied directly to the nature each of us possesses since we were created in His image. Yes, God is holy and just, and when He created humanity, we bore this aspect of His image. The loss of the image of God through the sin of Adam and Eve in the garden is recorded throughout scripture, and the consequences of the fall have left this world as a place of suffering. This is where most current discussion of the image of God ends. But there is more, so much more! What is God's nature, and what does it mean to be created in the image of God? God is a Triune being! There was intimate fellowship shared between the persons of the Trinity. I would dare to say that for most people today, if they even believe in God, He is viewed as harsh and, for the most part, uncaring.

For most Christians, the Father assumes this role. He is sitting on His throne, ready to judge and punish each of us when we step out of line. The proverbial lightning bolt from heaven. The attention of modern Christendom has shifted away from the Father to the Son. He is viewed as an obedient Son who did what the Father commanded and is fully subservient to the Father in everything. He is the One filled with compassion and love for humanity. After all, He is the one Who died for the sins of the world. The Holy Spirit is typically viewed in one of two ways. He is either an impersonal force of God who is acknowledged as a person of the Trinity but devoid of any personality, or the Spirit becomes the all-consuming focus Who must be demonstrably present in a person's life if the person is truly saved. There is, therefore, the view of God the Father as the One with all the true power and authority Who dictates to the other two, Who in turn do as they are commanded. Since they do the Father's will perfectly, we can trust in them and have hope for salvation because they are obedient when we fail.

Oh, how far we have fallen in our understanding of who God is and what He is truly like. It would do all of us a great service if we set aside everything we ever learned about God and begin to rethink Who He is according to how He has actually revealed Himself. So, what do we actually, factually know? God is Trinity, three persons who are together one God. Within this relationship, the three, Who are one in intent and purpose, do not seek to reign over each other, but rather they yield to one another out of love for each other. It is not that the Father dominates and dictates to the Son and the Spirit what They are to do, but rather that the Son and the Spirit joyfully yield to the heart of the Father and desire to do what pleases Him. So also, the Father has His heart set on loving the Son and honoring Him. It is the same for the Father and the Son Who live in relation with the Spirit. There is no structure of authority but rather mutual submission to the heart of each other. Again, it is not authority but mutual submission. It is not authority and power which mark the relationship of Father, Son, and Holy Spirit. It is love that binds them together and moves them to act in such a way as to be a blessing to each other. This mystery, this love, which is manifest in the relationship within the Trinity, is the image in which we were created. Adam was not created to dominate or be dominated by anyone; in fact, as the one who bore God's image, he was to have dominion over creation itself.

Examine the account of creation revealed in Genesis Chapter 1

Then God said, "Let us make man in our image, after our likeness. And let them have dominion over the fish of the sea and over the birds of the heavens and over the livestock and over all the earth and over every creeping thing that creeps on the earth." So God created man in his own image, in the image of God he created him; male and female he created them. And God blessed them. And God said to them, "Be fruitful and multiply and fill the earth and subdue it, and have dominion over the fish of the sea and over the birds of the heavens and over every living thing that moves on the earth." (Gen. 1:26-28 ESV)

It is important to note that there are no discrepancies between Genesis chapter one and chapter two. There are those who attempt to divide these two chapters and declare there were two different accounts of creation as if God did a reboot when the first one did not work out. What we see in these two chapters is actually a writing technique that is not uncommon today. Chapter one of Genesis gives us an overview of all of creation. Each day of creation is outlined, including the sixth day, the creation of both Adam and Eve.

When Moses moves beyond chapter one, he then retells the events of creation, focusing in detail on the sixth day, which was the primary purpose for all creation: human beings. So, chapter two of Genesis is a retelling of the most important aspects of chapter one.

What Does It Mean To Be Given Dominion

What is important to understand is that both man and woman were created by God and given dominion over all creation. While there is an order of creation that will be discussed later in this book, it was not that man was to dominate the woman, but they were to serve side by side in their dominion of creation. *"I will make a 'helper' suitable..."* is a special word in Hebrew that is used 21 times in the Old Testament, most often (16 times) of God being a 'helper' to His people. This further strengthens the idea that both men and women are made in the image of God equally, with different aspects of God's attributes in each one of them. However, the key question for our understanding is the meaning of "dominion."

What does it mean for Adam and Eve and each of us, as their descendants, to have dominion over all the earth? What does "dominion" actually mean? In our world today, many people confuse the definitions of dominion and dominate. Some even approach Scripture with the idea that these two words are synonymous. This confusion, set alongside a misreading of Genesis chapters one and two, has been the cause of horrific abuse in our world. When men or a man believes he is to dominate a woman or when human beings see it as their role to dominate creation itself, much damage is done. The word "dominate" has at its core the idea of control. The person who dominates lives life from the perspective that authority and control are the callings that have been placed upon their life. They are the boss, and it is their responsibility to ensure everyone follows the rules laid down and to enforce the consequences for those who disobey. This has led to great dysfunction in the family unit as women and children are made to live in fear of the man present in the household. It is also the attitude that has caused the rape and pillaging of nature and the natural resources of our world.

The understanding of "dominion" is vastly different. When God entrusted to Adam and Eve the dominion of the earth, it was the entrusting of a gift from God to His children. Dominion is not about power and control but rather care and responsibility. Dominion carries with it the idea of "stewardship." Creation itself was entrusted to humanity to care for and manage. The roles of a man and a woman, with different aspects of the image of God in each, are intended to enhance this care of creation so that all aspects of that care are included since each has a slightly different perspective. It was not given to us to use and abuse. This understanding of what was given in Genesis chapter one has far-reaching implications. A man is to have dominion over his wife. Not domination but dominion. This means the woman given to him is in his care to love, nurture, provide for, and protect. Dominion is about love and obedience (responsibility), not authority and control. Jesus Himself has dominion over all the earth as our God and Creator. What do we see in His life? Creation was His responsibility, and therefore He entered this world not as One who would demand His way but as One who would give of Himself to be faithful and to bless His creation.

This is the meaning behind the relationship of husband and wife in Ephesians chapter 5.

> *"Submitting to one another out of reverence for Christ. Wives, to your own husbands, as to the Lord. For the husband is the head of the wife even as Christ is the head of the church, his body, and is himself its Savior. Now as the church submits to Christ, so also wives should submit in everything to their husbands. Husbands, love your wives, as Christ loved the church and gave himself up for her, that he might sanctify her, having cleansed her by the washing*

> *of water with the word, so that he might present the church to himself in splendor, without spot or wrinkle or any such thing, that she might be holy and without blemish. In the same way husbands should love their wives as their own bodies. He who loves his wife loves himself. For no one ever hated his own flesh, but nourishes and cherishes it, just as Christ does the church, because we are members of his body."* (Eph. 5:21-30)

In this context, submission is not something that is forced, but rather a wife submits to the dominion of the husband because he is committed to doing what is best for her, even to the point of sacrificing himself so that she may be the one blessed. Dominion is at the heart of a relationship of agape love. Following the example given to us by Christ, a husband sets aside all his personal desires and chooses to do what is best for the one he loves, precisely because he loves. Eve was not created to be subservient to Adam but rather to be the focal point of his love. Eve was created to live in a relationship of love with Adam, and in so living, they would reveal the nature of God's image more fully. In the context of Genesis chapters one and two, Adam and Eve were given dominion over all creation, and together they were to oversee and make choices that were guided by love and which would result in the blessing of others. These choices were to be made based on love, even if a choice made meant doing what was best for others and not for themselves.

CHAPTER TWO

HUMANS ARE CREATED AS TRINITARIAN BEINGS BODY – SOUL – SPIRIT

For Christians, who believe they are created in the image of God, it is the Godhead, diversity in unity, and the three-in-oneness of God, which we and all creation reflect.

– Desmond Tutu

Let us return to our focus on God. If God is Trinity, the Three in One, and this is the very nature of His being, then would it not make sense that if God created mankind in His image, then mankind would be trinity as well? Throughout the centuries of the early church, up through the Middle Ages, and to the Reformation, it was understood that man was a three-part being. Created in the image of God, human beings are body, soul, and spirit. A more recent development in theology combines the soul and spirit and makes the terms synonymous. The question which must be answered is this; Is man a two-part being (Dichotomy) or a three-part being (Trichotomy)? The current understanding propagated within Christendom today is that man is a two-part being. Man is comprised of the body and the soul/spirit. This understanding approaches Scripture with the belief that the terms spirit and soul when referring to man are interchangeable.

Yet when we fully examine Scripture, we see God revealing something different and something much deeper. We turn to the Word of God to seek to correct this misunderstanding by presenting what Scripture teaches concerning each part of a human being: the spirit of a human being, the soul of a human being, and the body of a human being. It is this Trichotomy of the human being that reveals a fuller understanding of God creating man in His image. This understanding also opens the way to a fuller realization of the relationship God desires.

Two key passages for our consideration are the following:

> *For the word of God is living and active, sharper than any two-edged sword, piercing to the division of soul and of spirit, of joints and of marrow, and discerning the thoughts and intentions of the heart.* Hebrews 4:12
> *Now may the God of peace himself sanctify you completely, and may your whole spirit and soul and body be kept blameless at the coming of our Lord Jesus Christ.*
> 1 Thessalonians 5:23

In these two passages, there is a distinction made between the spirit of a human being and the person's soul. In each passage, God is working to accomplish His purposes.

The Hebrew and Greek words which are primary to this study are the following:

Note: The two primary languages utilized by God in the Bible are vastly different. Hebrew, which is the primary language of the Old Testament, is a "picture" language. It is filled with multiple images and thoughts, which are used to build upon each other to form a symbolic picture.

The Greek language, in which the New Testament was written, is a very precise language. There are often multiple words with varied nuances of meaning for the same topic.

Therefore, the Old Testament paints a picture of human beings as body, soul, and spirit with very broad-brush strokes, and the New Testament addresses the same aspects of human beings in very precise terms.

In order to more fully understand the truths which Scripture reveals, we will take the time to examine each Hebrew and Greek word referencing body, soul, and spirit, and then apply this understanding to the Word of God in search of clarity.

The Words For Body

In what ways do the Scriptures use the word body (flesh) in reference to man?

In Hebrew, the word is Basar (בָּשָׂר) In each of the following passages, basar is used:

Genesis 2:21   So the LORD God caused a deep sleep to fall upon the man, and while he slept took one of his ribs and closed up its place with <u>flesh</u> *Basar* (בָּשָׂר).

Genesis 6:3 — Then the LORD said, "My Spirit shall not abide in man forever, for he is <u>flesh</u> *Basar* (בָּשָׂר): his days shall be 120 years."

Genesis 6:19 — And of every living thing of all <u>flesh</u> *Basar* (בָּשָׂר), you shall bring two of every sort into the ark to keep them alive with you. They shall be male and female.

Genesis 9:4 — But you shall not eat <u>flesh</u> *Basar* (בָּשָׂר) with its life, that is, its blood.

(This passage contains both Basar (בָּשָׂר) and nephesh (נֶפֶשׁ). "You shall not eat the basar with its nephesh, that is, its blood or lifeblood." What is translated into English as blood or lifeblood is actually the Hebrew word for soul. In this passage, even the animals are depicted as having a "soul." (A unique identity with mind, will, and emotions.)

Job 12:10 — In his hand is the life of every living thing and the breath of all <u>mankind</u> *Basar* (בָּשָׂר).

(This passage, like the preceding, contains both words depicting all living things, both man and animals have flesh and soul. There is no mention of spirit in these two passages.)

Ezekiel 36:26 — And I will give you a new heart, and a new spirit I will put within you. And I will remove the heart of stone from your <u>flesh</u> *Basar* (בָּשָׂר) and give you a heart of <u>flesh</u> *Basar* (בָּשָׂר).

(In this passage, the new heart will be given when a new spirit (Ruach) is placed within man.)

Zech 2:13　　Be silent, all <u>flesh</u> *Basar* (בָשָׂר), before the LORD, for he has roused himself from his holy dwelling.

Leviticus 22:6　　The person who touches such a thing shall be unclean until the evening and shall not eat of the holy things unless he has bathed his <u>body</u> *Basar* (בָשָׂר) in water.

Job 14:22　　He feels only the pain of his own <u>body</u> *Basar* (בָשָׂר), and he mourns only for himself."

Psalm 31:9　　Be gracious to me, O LORD, for I am in distress; my eye is wasted from grief; my soul *nephesh* (נֶפֶשׁ) and my <u>body</u> *Basar* (בָשָׂר) also.

(In this passage, David cries out to God because both his soul and body are stricken with grief.)

In New Testament Greek, one word is Soma (σῶμα)

Matt 5:29　　If your right eye causes you to sin, tear it out and throw it away. For it is better that you lose one of your members than that your whole <u>body</u> *Soma* (σῶμα) be thrown into hell.

Matt 6:22　　"The eye is the lamp of the <u>body</u> *Soma* (σῶμα). So, if your eye is healthy, your whole <u>body</u> *Soma* (σῶμα) will be full of light,

Mark 14:8　　She has done what she could; she has anointed my <u>body</u> *Soma* (σῶμα) beforehand for burial.

Luke 12:4	"I tell you, my friends, do not fear those who kill the <u>body</u> *Soma* (σῶμα), and after that have nothing more that they can do.
Romans 6:6	We know that our old self was crucified with him in order that the <u>body</u> *Soma* (σῶμα) of sin might be brought to nothing, so that we would no longer be enslaved to sin.
Romans 8:10	But if Christ is in you, although the <u>body</u> *Soma* (σῶμα) is dead because of sin, the Spirit is life because of righteousness.
Phil 3:21	Who will transform our lowly <u>body</u> *Soma* (σῶμα) to be like his glorious <u>body</u> *Soma* (σῶμα), by the power that enables him even to subject all things to himself.
Heb 10:22	Let us draw near with a true heart in full assurance of faith, with our hearts sprinkled clean from an evil conscience and our <u>bodies</u> *Soma* (σῶμα) washed with pure water.
James 3:3	If we put bits into the mouths of horses so that they obey us, we guide their whole <u>bodies</u> *Soma* (σῶμα) as well.
Matt 27:52	The tombs also were opened. And many <u>bodies</u> *Soma* (σῶμα) of the saints who had fallen asleep were raised,
Matt 27:58	He went to Pilate and asked for the <u>body</u> *Soma* (σῶμα) of Jesus. Then Pilate ordered it to be given to him.
Acts 9:40	But Peter put them all outside, and knelt down and prayed; and turning to the <u>body</u> *Soma* (σῶμα) he said,

"Tabitha, arise." And she opened her eyes, and when she saw Peter, she sat up.

The second word in Greek is Sarx (σάρξ)

Matt 19:6	So they are no longer two but one <u>flesh</u> *Sarx* (σάρξ). What therefore God has joined together, let not man separate."
Matt 24:22	And if those days had not been cut short, no <u>human being</u> (flesh) *Sarx* (σάρξ) would be saved. But for the sake of the elect those days will be cut short.
Matt 26:41	Watch and pray that you may not enter into temptation. The spirit indeed is willing, but the <u>flesh</u> *Sarx* (σάρξ) is weak."
John 1:14	And the Word became <u>flesh</u> *Sarx* (σάρξ) and dwelt among us, and we have seen his glory, glory as of the only Son from the Father, full of grace and truth.
John 3:6	That which is born of the <u>flesh</u> *Sarx* (σάρξ) is <u>flesh</u> *Sarks* (σάρξ) and that which is born of the Spirit is spirit.
John 6:51	I am the living bread that came down from heaven. If anyone eats of this bread, he will live forever. And the bread that I will give for the life of the world is my <u>flesh</u> *Sarx* (σάρξ)."
Acts 2:26	Therefore my heart was glad, and my tongue rejoiced; my <u>flesh</u> *Sarx* (σάρξ) also will dwell in hope.

Acts 2:31   He foresaw and spoke about the resurrection of the Christ, that he was not abandoned to Hades, nor did his <u>flesh</u> *Sarx* (σάρξ) see corruption.

Romans 3:20   For by works of the law no <u>human being</u> *Sarks* (σάρξ) will be justified in his sight, since through the law comes knowledge of sin.

1 Peter 1:24   For "All <u>flesh</u> *Sarx* (σάρξ) is like grass and all its glory like the flower of grass. The grass withers, and the flower falls.

The Greek word for "body" is **Soma** (σῶμα) the physical body of persons, animals, or plants, either dead or alive. πάντα δὲ τὰ μέλη τοῦ σώματος πολλὰ ὄντα ἕν ἐστιν σῶμα "though all the parts of the body are many, it is still one body" (1 Corinthians 12:12); ὅπου τὸ σῶμά ἐκεῖ καὶ οἱ ἀετοὶ ἐπισυναχθήσονται "where there is a body, the vultures will gather" (Luke 17:37); οὐ τὸ σῶμα τὸ γενησόμενον σπείρεις "you do not sow the body of the plant which is to be" (1 Corinthians 15:37).

In a number of languages, a clear distinction must be made between the body of a living person and a dead body (or corpse). Other languages distinguish between the bodies of persons and the bodies of animals, and frequently the term for a body of a plant is distinct from those referring to persons or animals. Often a term for body consists of a phrase, for example, "flesh and bones," and in several languages, a reference to the body is made primarily by referring to the person himself. For example, in Matthew 26:13; *"has poured this ointment on my body,"* the appropriate equivalent may be *"has poured this ointment on me."* In certain instances, "body" may be rendered as something which is experienced. For example, in 1 Corinthians 6:20; *"glorify God through your body"* may be rendered as *"glorify God through what you do"* or *"... do in your body."*

Sarx σάρξ σαρκός: the flesh of both animals and human beings - 'flesh.' δεῦτε᾽᾽᾽ ἵνα φάγητε σάρκας βασιλέων᾽᾽᾽ καὶ σάρκας ἵππων *"come ... and eat the flesh of kings ... and the flesh of horses."* Revelation 19:17-18. Some languages, however, make an important distinction between the flesh of a living person and the flesh of someone who has been killed or who has died. It would be this latter sense which should be reflected in Revelation 19:18. Conversely, in Romans 2:28, the reference to 'circumcision in the flesh' (ἐν σαρκὶ περιτομη,) would, however, require the first sense, namely, the flesh of a living person.

The Words For Soul

In what ways do the Scriptures use the word soul when referring to the human soul? (Hebrew (נֶפֶשׁ) nephesh and Greek (ψύχει) psyche).

Nephesh used to refer to life in general or the life of a person

Genesis 1:30   And to every beast of the earth and to every bird of the heavens and to everything that creeps on the earth, everything that has the <u>breath of life</u> *Nephesh* (נֶפֶשׁ), I have given every green plant for food." And it was so.

Genesis 2:19   Now out of the ground the LORD God had formed every beast of the field and every bird of the heavens and brought them to the man to see what he would call them.

And whatever the man called every living *Nephesh* (נֶפֶשׁ) creature, that was its name.

Genesis 2:7   then the LORD God formed the man of dust from the ground and breathed into his nostrils the breath of life, and the man became a living *Nephesh* (נֶפֶשׁ) creature, (nephesh).

Exodus 31:14 You shall keep the Sabbath, because it is holy for you. Everyone who profanes it shall be put to death. Whoever does any work on it, that soul *Nephesh* (נֶפֶשׁ) shall be cut off from among his people.

Genesis 37:21 But when Reuben heard it, he rescued him out of their hands, saying, "Let us not take his life *Nephesh* (נֶפֶשׁ)."

Exodus 21:23 But if there is harm, then you shall pay life *Nephesh* (נֶפֶשׁ), for life *Nephesh* (נֶפֶשׁ).

Nephesh used to identify the will and/or emotions of a person.

OLD TESTAMENT Hebrew (נֶפֶשׁ) nephesh.

Genesis 34:3 And his soul *Nephesh* (נֶפֶשׁ) was drawn to Dinah the daughter of Jacob. He loved the young woman and spoke tenderly to her.

Lev 26:15   If you spurn my statutes, and if your soul *Nephesh* (נֶפֶשׁ) abhors my rules, so that you will not do all my commandments, but break my covenant,

Deut 4:9	"Only take care, and keep your <u>soul</u> *Nephesh* (נֶפֶשׁ) diligently, lest you forget the things that your eyes have seen, and lest they depart from your heart all the days of your life. Make them known to your children and your children's children--
Deut 4:29	But from there you will seek the LORD your God and you will find him, if you search after him with all your heart and with all your <u>soul</u> *Nephesh* (נֶפֶשׁ).
Deut 6:5	You shall love the LORD your God with all your heart and with all your <u>soul</u> *Nephesh* (נֶפֶשׁ) and with all your might.
Judges 16:16	And when she pressed him hard with her words day after day, and urged him, his <u>soul</u> *Nephesh* (נֶפֶשׁ) was vexed to death.
Job 30:16	"And now my <u>soul</u> *Nephesh* (נֶפֶשׁ) is poured out within me; days of affliction have taken hold of me.
Job 30:25	Did not I weep for him whose day was hard? Was not my <u>soul</u> *Nephesh* (נֶפֶשׁ) grieved for the needy?
Psalm 6:3	My <u>soul</u> *Nephesh* (נֶפֶשׁ) also is greatly troubled. But you, O LORD--how long?
Psalm 23:3	He restores my <u>soul</u> *Nephesh* (נֶפֶשׁ). He leads me in paths of righteousness for his name's sake.

Psalm 56:13   For you have delivered my <u>soul</u> *Nephesh* (נֶפֶשׁ) from death, yes, my feet from falling, that I may walk before God in the light of life.

Because the Hebrew language is not as precise as the Greek but instead creates symbols or pictures for our understanding, it might be helpful not to attempt a hard and fast distinction between "ruach" (רוּחַ) and "nephesh" (נֶפֶשׁ) as we seek to establish in the Greek.

The "ruach" spirit is necessary for the "nephesh" soul to exist. The "breath of life" must be present for there to be "life" present. All of this takes place in the "basar" (בָּשָׂר), the body. Many of the attributes seem to cross over between "nephesh" and "ruach," which makes a clear distinction extremely difficult.

NEW TESTAMENT Greek (ψύχει) psyche or soul.

Luke 12:20   But God said to him, 'Fool! This night your <u>soul</u> *Psyche* (ψύχει) is required of you, and the things you have prepared, whose will they be?'

Matt 20:28   Even as the Son of Man came not to be served but to serve, and to give his <u>life</u> *Psyche* (ψύχει) as a ransom for many."

Mark 12:30   And you shall love the Lord your God with all your heart and with all your <u>soul</u> *Psyche* (ψύχει) and with all your mind and with all your strength.'

Acts 15:26   men who have risked their <u>lives</u> *Psyche* (ψύχει) for the sake of our Lord Jesus Christ.

Luke 1:46	And Mary said, "My <u>soul</u> *Psyche* (ψύχει) magnifies the Lord.
Acts 2:43	And awe came upon every <u>soul</u> *Psyche* (ψύχει), and many wonders and signs were being done through the apostles.
Ephesians 6:6	Not by the way of eye-service, as people-pleasers, but as servants of Christ, doing the will of God from the <u>heart</u> *Psyche* (ψύχει).
1 Peter 2:11	Beloved, I urge you as sojourners and exiles to abstain from the passions of the flesh, which wage war against your <u>soul</u> *Psyche* (ψύχει).

In the context of these and many other passages we see ψύχει (psyche - soul) used with reference to the soul of a man which can respond to circumstances of life with great emotion, and which can also be sacrificed or taken, i.e., Death.

The Words For Spirit

In what ways do the Scriptures use the word spirit when referring to the spirit of a human being? ("ruach" (רוּחַ) and (πνεῦμα) "pneuma").

OLD TESTAMENT **"ruach"** (רוּחַ)

Psalm 32:2	Blessed is the man against whom the LORD counts no iniquity, and in whose <u>spirit</u> *Ruach* (רוּחַ) there is no deceit.

Job 20:3   "I listened to the reproof which insults me, And the spirit *Ruach* (רוּחַ) of my understanding makes me answer.

Psalm 51:10   Create in me a clean heart, O God, and renew a right spirit *Ruach* (רוּחַ) within me.

Proverbs 17:22 A joyful heart is good medicine, but a crushed spirit *Ruach* (רוּחַ) dries up the bones.

Proverbs 18:14 A man's spirit *Ruach* (רוּחַ) will endure sickness, but a crushed spirit who can bear?

Ezekiel 3:14   The Spirit lifted me up and took me away, and I went in bitterness in the heat of my spirit *Ruach* (רוּחַ), the hand of the LORD being strong upon me.

Isaiah 26:9   My soul yearns for you in the night; my spirit *Ruach* (רוּחַ) within me earnestly seeks you. For when your judgments are in the earth, the inhabitants of the world learn righteousness.

Daniel 5:20   But when his heart was lifted up and his spirit *Ruach* (רוּחַ) was hardened so that he dealt proudly, he was brought down from his kingly throne, and his glory was taken from him.

Zec. 12:1   The burden of the word of the LORD concerning Israel: Thus declares the LORD, who stretched out the heavens and founded the earth and formed the spirit *Ruach* (רוּחַ) of man within him:

Ecc. 12:7   And the dust returns to the earth as it was, and the <u>spirit</u> *Ruach* (רוּחַ) returns to God who gave it.

In each of the preceding passages, the "spirit" of a person "ruach" (רוּחַ) is identified as that part of a person who lives in relation to God or suffers from the brokenness of sin.

NEW TESTAMENT "pneuma" (πνεῦμα)

Matt 5:3   "Blessed are the poor in <u>spirit</u> *Pneuma* (πνεῦμα), for theirs is the kingdom of heaven.

Matt 26:41   Watch and pray that you may not enter into temptation. The <u>spirit</u> *Pneuma* (πνεῦμα) indeed is willing, but the flesh is weak."

Luke 1:47   And my <u>spirit</u> *Pneuma* (πνεῦμα) rejoices in God my Savior.

John 4:23   But the hour is coming, and is now here, when the true worshipers will worship the Father in <u>spirit</u> *Pneuma* (πνεῦμα) and truth, for the Father is seeking such people to worship him.

Romans 1:9   For God is my witness, whom I serve with my <u>spirit</u> *Pneuma* (πνεῦμα) in the gospel of his Son, that without ceasing I mention you.

Romans 8:16   The Spirit himself bears witness with our <u>spirit</u> *Pneuma* (πνεῦμα) that we are children of God,

Phil 4:23	The grace of the Lord Jesus Christ be with your <u>spirit</u> *Pneuma* (πνεῦμα).
Luke 8:55	And her <u>spirit</u> *Pneuma* (πνεῦμα) returned, and she got up at once. And he directed that something should be given her to eat.
James 2:26	For as the body apart from the <u>spirit</u> *Pneuma* (πνεῦμα) is dead, so also faith apart from works is dead.
Rom 12:11	Do not be slothful in zeal, be fervent in <u>spirit</u> *Pneuma* (πνεῦμα), serve the Lord.
1 Cor 2:11	For who knows a person's thoughts except the <u>spirit</u> *Pneuma* (πνεῦμα) of that person, which is in him? So also no one comprehends the thoughts of God except the Spirit of God.
1 Cor 5:5	You are to deliver this man to Satan for the destruction of the flesh, so that his <u>spirit</u> *Pneuma* (πνεῦμα) may be saved in the day of the Lord.
1 Cor 7:34	and his interests are divided. And the unmarried or betrothed woman is anxious about the things of the Lord, how to be holy in body and <u>spirit</u> *Pneuma* (πνεῦμα). But the married woman is anxious about worldly things, how to please her husband.
1 Cor 14:14	For if I pray in a tongue, my <u>spirit</u> *Pneuma* (πνεῦμα) prays but my mind is unfruitful.

1 Cor 14:15	What am I to do? I will pray with my spirit *Pneuma* (πνεῦμα), but I will pray with my mind also; I will sing praise with my spirit *Pneuma* (πνεῦμα), but I will sing with my mind also.
2 Cor 7:1	Since we have these promises, beloved, let us cleanse ourselves from every defilement of body and spirit *Pneuma* (πνεῦμα), bringing holiness to completion in the fear of God.
Gal 6:18	The grace of our Lord Jesus Christ be with your spirit *Pneuma* (πνεῦμα), brothers.
Eph 4:23	And to be renewed in the spirit *Pneuma* (πνεῦμα) of your minds.
James 4:5	Or do you suppose it is to no purpose that the Scripture says, "He yearns jealously over the spirit *Pneuma* (πνεῦμα) that he has made to dwell in us"?

There are many passages in the New Testament which use the word **"pneuma"** with reference to the Holy Spirit. The preceding passages were selected precisely because they reference the "spirit" of a human being as a person lives in relationship with God.

CHAPTER THREE

THE HUMAN SPIRIT IS CREATED BY GOD

"The Spirit of God has made me, And the breath of the Almighty gives me life."

— Job 33:4

With all we have revealed to us in Scripture, what are we able to glean and understand? Solomon is declared to be the wisest man who ever lived. When he was made king of Israel, God asked what he desired. He could have asked for anything, but he asked for wisdom. The account is given to us in 1 Kings.

Now, O LORD my God, You have made Your servant king in place of my father David, yet I am but a little child; I do not know how to go out or come in. Your servant is in the midst of Your people which You have chosen, a great people who are too many to be numbered or counted. So give Your servant an understanding heart to judge Your people to discern between good and evil. For who is able to judge this great people of Yours? It was pleasing in the sight

> *of the Lord that Solomon had asked this thing. God said to him, "Because you have asked this thing and have not asked for yourself long life, nor have asked riches for yourself, nor have you asked for the life of your enemies, but have asked for yourself discernment to understand justice, behold, I have done according to your words. Behold, I have given you a wise and discerning heart, so that there has been no one like you before you, nor shall one like you arise after you.* (1 Ki. 3:7-12)

As one who was given wisdom from God, Solomon understood not only life in this world, but he was given to know God in a unique way. He could understand more clearly how God works in us and among us to bless us. He writes of love and life in this world. He writes of what it means to live in a world where we grow older day by day. Solomon is known for using allegory or symbolism to describe in a picture language what each subject he addresses means to us. Certainly, the Song of Solomon depicts the love between a man and a woman in a way that is unparalleled in any other written literature. It is in Ecclesiastes where Solomon uses images familiar to each of us to describe what it means to grow older and the effect of age on the human body. In his final words of Ecclesiastes at the very end of chapter 12, he makes the following statement.

> *Then the dust will return to the earth as it was, and the spirit will return to God who gave it.* (Ecclesiastes 12:7)

The reference to "dust" is from the account in the garden when God tells Adam that he was created from the dust of the earth and that when death comes to him because of his sin, he will return to the dust. Solomon understood the future of the physical body of every human being ever born into this world. He also understood the "spirit" of a person and what God has done and will do in the future. When Solomon states that *the spirit will return to God, who gave it,* he is giving us an understanding of God's ongoing involvement in creation. When a man and woman come together, and a child is conceived, the resulting child, body and soul, are the result of the DNA contributed by the mother and the father.

Human beings are not able to create an eternal spirit! This means that every child created has God working to create the human spirit of that child. God's purpose is to create the human spirit to know Him and live in a relationship with Him in this life, and once this life is over, to return to Him and dwell in His presence forever. God is still a creating God, Who is intimately involved in creation. There has never been born a child who was an accident or a child who was unloved by God. God creates for the purpose of relationship, which means you were created to live in a relationship with the God who created you!

It is, therefore, to be understood that the spirit of a human being is created by God at conception and, in that instant, joined to the body as the part of a human being which is created to live in fellowship with God by His grace. It is this invisible and immaterial part of a person which will live beyond life in this world, either with God (the believer) or in judgment (the unbeliever), until the day of resurrection when it will be reunited with an immortal body.

Each aspect of a human being has a unique function yet exists in unity with the whole.

What are the functions of the Spirit, Soul, and Body in a person?

What is the body? basar (בָּשָׂר) soma ($\sigma\tilde{\omega}\mu\alpha$) sarx ($\sigma\acute{\alpha}\rho\xi$)

Through the examination of the previous Scripture passages in which the various terms *basar*, *sarx*, and *soma* are used, it is clear that the human body is the physical aspect of humans.

The body is the place of the indwelling of both the human spirit and soul. When the spirit is present in the body, the soul is then present, as seen in what we can call the personality of the person. When the spirit is absent from the body, the soul ceases to exist, and this is generally referred to as a corpse.

The human body is the first identifying aspect of a human being. When we encounter a person, it is the body, i.e., the physical aspects, to which we immediately relate to. Upon entering into a relationship, we immediately begin to relate beyond the physical to the level of the soul.

While the body could be deemed as only the "shell" or "husk" for what is vastly more important, soul and spirit, it is the vehicle of both sin and performing God's will. The body was created by God and is loved by Him. Jesus came not only to redeem a person's spirit but also to redeem the whole person -- spirit, soul, and body.

While our bodies are corrupted by the fall into sin and therefore plagued with both the cravings and consequences of sin, the day of resurrection will reveal the true desire of God. All believers shall receive a resurrected and glorified body, free from every aspect of sin.

What is the soul? (Hebrew (נֶפֶשׁ) nephesh and Greek (ψύχει) psyche)

We learn from the Word of God that all living things, both humans and animals, have a soul. The soul of a living being is what is encountered beyond the physical level. Soul is defined as the heart of a person, the mind, will, emotions, desires, appetites, etc. We can understand this as the personality of a living being. Be it a person or an animal, we understand that each is a unique soul.

The soul of any living being is influenced by its surroundings. If a person is harsh and cruel to a dog, the dog will develop a personality that is either aggressive or cowardly. What can be said of an animal is also true for humans. Some are gentle, and some are harsh.

The soul manifests itself in the body giving life and uniqueness to each one. Apart from the work of God, the human soul is driven by sinful desires and lives life in the flesh, seeking to satisfy itself. Through the work of the Holy Spirit giving new birth to the spirit of a person, a new direction is given for life. This new life given by the Holy Spirit gives new direction to the human spirit and therefore influences a person's soul to live according to God's will.

What is the human spirit? ("ruach" (רוּחַ) and (πνεῦμα) "pneuma")

The human spirit is unique to human beings. It is what sets humans apart from all other living creatures. The spirit of a person is that part which God has created, and which is intended to live in relationship with Him. The spirit of a person, once created by God, will live forever. It is to be understood that the flesh will also live forever after the day of resurrection. When a person dies, the body returns to the dust of the ground, but the spirit continues to live.

While the soul is the seat of desire and emotions, it is the spirit that seeks to live in a relationship with God. In the absence of the Holy Spirit, the human spirit seeks spiritual things in all manner of places.

Through the work of the Holy Spirit, the human spirit is given faith by which all the promises of God are believed. Faith present in the spirit enables a person to believe in Christ as Savior, live in a true relationship with God the Father, and then work through the soul to live a Christ-like life.

CHAPTER FOUR

LIFE WITH GOD BEFORE AND AFTER THE FALL INTO SIN

"There is an old joke that went around- it goes, in the beginning God made man in His own image, and since the fall, man has been seeking to return the compliment."

– Alistair Begg

Adam's relationship with God before the fall into sin.

Genesis 1:26 - 2:1 *Then God said, "Let us make man in our image, after our likeness. And let them have dominion over the fish of the sea and over the birds of the heavens and over the livestock and over all the earth and over every creeping thing that creeps on the earth." 27 So God created man in his own image, in the image of God he created him; male and female he created them. 28 And God blessed them. And God said to them, "Be fruitful and multiply and fill the earth and subdue it and have dominion over the fish of the sea and over the birds of the heavens and over every living thing that moves on the earth." 29 And God said, "Behold, I have given you every plant yielding seed that is on the face of all the earth, and every tree with seed in its fruit. You shall have them for food. 30 And to every beast of the earth and to every bird of the heavens and to everything that creeps on the earth, everything that has the breath of life, I have given every green plant for food." And it was so. 31 And God saw everything that he had made, and behold, it was very good. And there was evening and there was morning, the sixth day.*

In the garden, all was created by God for Adam. Adam was blessed to live in true harmony with all creation and his Creator.

Genesis 2:7-8 then the LORD God formed the man of dust from the ground and breathed into his nostrils the breath of life, and the man became a living creature. 8 And the LORD God planted a garden in Eden, in the east, and there he put the man whom he had formed.

Scripture reveals a broad overview of creation in Genesis chapter 1 but then retells the primary focus of creation in chapter 2. Chapter 1 reveals God as the Creator, while chapter 2 reveals that God created everything for humans. Creation was intended to be God's gift to mankind.

Unlike what is revealed for all of creation in general, the creation of Adam shows the great care God took in creating him and the uniqueness of the image of God he bore. This uniqueness is also seen in the life God gave him as He breathed into his nostrils the breath of life. This action of God is not revealed to have taken place for any of the animals; it is unique to Adam.

When God created man, what set him apart from the animal kingdom was that once God had formed man's body, He breathed into his nostrils the "breath of life." The pressing question is this, what did God do for man at that moment which set him apart from all other created life?

What was it which God breathed into the lifeless form of a man which brought life? Once this breathing into the nostrils of the man took place, Genesis 2:7 declares that "the man became a living soul (being). What did God add to the creation of man, which was absent from the creation of animals?

In order to understand what is taking place in the text, it is necessary to examine other texts to gain a fuller understanding. One story to turn our attention to is the account of Elijah raising the widow's son in 1 Kings 17. Elijah took the lifeless body of the child to an upper room. There he laid the child down, and according to the text, Elijah stretched himself out on the child three times. The Septuagint, which is the ancient Greek translation of the Old Testament, uses the word *"breathed"* on the child three times. The image is of Elijah placing himself on the child, hand to hand, face to face, mouth to mouth, and when this had been done three times, he cried out to God, *"return the life of this child to him."* It appears that in the same way God breathed into the man's nostrils the "breath of life," Elijah copied God's actions in ,this child's life, asking that this child be restored. If we understand that we are each body, soul, and spirit, created as triune beings, then we also believe that when the spirit of a person is absent from the body, there is no life present. Elijah is asking God to restore the spirit of this child so that life may be returned. It is impossible for a human being to have life in the absence of spirit, for all that is left is the body, which is the vessel of the spirit.

Another text which adds to our understanding is found in John 20:22: *And when he had said this, he breathed on them and said to them, "Receive the Holy Spirit."* Jesus was doing more than simply exhaling on the disciples. Jesus breathed forth the Holy Spirit, and the Spirit was received by the Apostles. This is the same word used in the ancient Greek translation of the Genesis text when God breathed into the nostrils of the lifeless form of man. God breathes out, and His Spirit goes forth, and life is created. This was true for Adam in the Garden of Eden, and it was true for the Apostles when Jesus breathed the life-giving Spirit into them.

Solomon wrote in the book of Proverbs, "The spirit of man is the lamp of the LORD, searching all his innermost parts" (20:27). A more literal translation from Hebrew is as follows; *"The light of the Lord is the breath of man, searching all his innermost parts."* The breath of life in the garden was the life-giving Spirit of God which brings true life and relationship with God. In the absence of the Spirit of God, a human being is left empty, searching, and yearning for the life which once was. God had created people to live in a truly intimate relationship with Him, and it was the Spirit of God that both brought forth life from lifelessness and sustained this life-giving relationship.

The intimate relationship between Adam and God is seen in the declaration of God on the sixth day of creation that it was "very good." Life in the garden was not labor and toil! God declared this to be part of the curse of the fall into sin when Adam and Eve were expelled from the garden. Life in the garden, before the fall, is pictured as harvest time all the time. Adam lived in harmony with his wife and all creation and in harmony with God. In Genesis 3:10, Adam states to God, *"I heard the sound of you in the garden."* Adam was not surprised that God came into the garden. The implication seems to be that God came into the garden each day in the cool of the day.

What would we see if we could step back in time and imagine a family and what life would have been like apart from the Fall into sin? We would see two people, a man, and a woman, who love each other and whose love is full and complete but who yearn to express their love through the creation of life. A child is born, and then another and another. The family grows, and the journey toward maturity begins. Loving parents care for the vulnerable child and teach what is needed at each stage of development. Each child looks to both father and mother to gain the necessary understanding needed to grow. The father teaches his son what it means to become a man first by his example. A young boy sees his father as one who is dependable and faithful to his wife and family. He is the protector and provider of all they need. The daughter looks at her father and sees a man who is captivated by the beauty of his wife and loves her selflessly. Both a boy and a girl will see in their father the heart of a true man whose focus in life is to be a blessing to the ones he loves.

The same young boy will look to his mother as the one whose heart is filled with compassion for him. He will experience tenderness and encouragement from her as he grows, and he will be captivated by the selfless love she has for him. The young girl will see all these things in her mother, but it goes a step further. The young girl wants to be like her mother. She learns from her what it means to believe in and trust her husband. It is more than simply the skills needed to live as an adult that the girl learns, she learns her own value and worth in the eyes of another as she sees her mother cherished by her father. Together a father and mother reveal the image of God to their children through their relationship with each other, which is one of dominion and not dominance. This giving of oneself to bless the other, in turn, provides the greatest blessing for the children in the family.

This was what God intended for life in the Garden and in the whole world to be like. It is foundational to our understanding of life in the garden prior to the fall that we realize God created the Garden as a place to live in relationship with His children. God did not simply create and then step out of the picture. God was present and involved in His creation, having created all things so He might live in true intimate fellowship with people.

Adam's Relationship With God After The Fall

Once sin was conceived, it gave birth to death! (*Then desire, when it has conceived, gives birth to sin, and sin, when it is fully grown, brings forth death.* James 1:15). God had told Adam that on the day he ate the forbidden fruit, he would die. There are two types of death, spiritual and physical. When Adam and Eve ate from the tree, they immediately died a spiritual death. Spiritual death is not the absence of the human spirit or of spirituality. Spiritual death is the absence of the ability to live in relationship with God. The human spirit, which was created by God and unique to human beings, died a spiritual death. This means Adam and all humans after him could no longer live in harmony or relationship with their Creator. Adam was no longer able to stand in the presence of God and fellowship with Him. Instead, when he heard God walking in the garden, he ran away and hid himself.

In the banishment of Adam and Eve from the garden, we see not only the physical consequence of sin but also the spiritual consequences. Adam would work hard all his life and would eventually die a physical death. This consequence would come in time. The immediate consequence of spiritual death is seen in that Adam is sent from the garden, never again to be able to stand in God's presence or live in unity with Him.

The Existence Of Man Apart From God

Even after the fall into sin, human beings are still spiritual beings. The spirit "ruach" (רוּחַ) or ($\pi\nu\epsilon\hat{u}\mu\alpha$) "pneuma" of a human was created to live in relationship with God. But the result of sin has left all humans unable to live in this relationship. Sin has left all mankind blind to God and empty in spirit. The absence of a relationship with God has left all humans wandering and searching for what is missing. The "god-shaped hole in the heart of man" is the reality that a relationship with God is impossible for man to achieve. This search for the spiritual has led man to substitute false beliefs for true relationship. It was by his own actions that Adam sinned. It is now, by our own actions, that all human beings seek something to fill the spiritual void in their lives. Apart from the action of the Holy Spirit in the Gospel, mankind wanders into false beliefs.

The relationship created by God in the garden was by God's design. It was complete and fulfilling to Adam. This relationship is now gone, and all knowledge of the true God is veiled from human understanding. *(And even if our gospel is veiled, it is veiled to those who are perishing. In their case, the god of this world has blinded the minds of the unbelievers to keep them from seeing the light of the gospel of the glory of Christ, who is the image of God. 2 Corinthians 4:3-4),* because sinful humanity cannot comprehend the true God apart from Christ and the Gospel, we now substitute the false for the true by our own efforts.

False Religions - Why Do They Seem To Satisfy?

There are myriads of false religions and false beliefs present in the world. The one common denominator of all systems of belief, except Christianity, is that spiritual fulfillment can be obtained through a person's efforts. False religions meet a felt need in the heart of a sinful human being because they seem to fill the void left in the human spirit resulting from the absence of God.

They make sense to human beings.

The absence of a true relationship with God leaves human beings to substitute the "imaginations" (Acts 17:29) of their own beliefs for God. Creating a god in our own image allows each person to put god in a box which is what the apostle Paul addresses in Romans chapter one; *"For although they knew God, they did not honor him as God or give thanks to him, but they became futile in their thinking, and their foolish hearts were darkened. Claiming to be wise, they became fools and exchanged the glory of the immortal God for images resembling mortal man and birds and animals and creeping things"* (1:21-23).

Larger than man, but man can comprehend them.

The emptiness in the heart of each human being reveals to a person the reality that there is more to life than simple existence. There is something more! Something beyond the (נֶפֶשׁ) "nephesh" or ego! Something beyond self. At the same time, sin leads each person to the false belief that he does not need a God who is wholly "other" than himself but a spirituality or connection with the divine, which is attainable from within himself. Thus, the sinful imagination of each human being creates its own idea of god.

The history of the world is filled with examples of peoples and cultures who created systems of beliefs based on a god who reflected the qualities of human beings we see today in the 21st century. Because these gods were created in the image of man, they have been given the attributes of human beings, both good and bad.

Human beings are unable to relate to a God who is holy and, therefore, wholly beyond what we are. By the creation of a spiritual reality according to human design, individuals are able to relate to something beyond themselves, yet within their ability to grasp and control.

The human spirit seeks to reclaim what was lost by its own actions - Works appeal.

Each individual imagines god or their idea of spirituality, setting the conditions and limits of belief and what is necessary for acceptance or rejection by the divine. Since it was by human action (Adam's sin) that spiritual life with God was lost, it is therefore in the heart of all humans to seek to obtain what has been lost by our own actions.

Each person's belief system or each religion creates the necessary conditions by which a person is acceptable and the punishments for disobedience. If the belief system becomes too overbearing, many flee to a different belief system that is more attractive to the person, or they are left to despair.

The Illusion Of Progress

It is in the heart of every human being to seek God, but in the absence of any true understanding of Who God is or what He is truly like, each person imagines their god and sets the standard by which they can obtain either a relationship with this god or at least receive their god's approval.

There are many, in fact, most people who simply feel lost and unable to connect with God. There are others who have developed elaborate systems of beliefs and standards for people to find a feeling of comfort and/or assurance if they will wholly submit to the teachings presented. Those who have propagated false belief systems span the history of humanity. Some of the most notable in world history took the common elements of life in this broken world and elevated them to "god" status, and directed people to bow down before them.

For example, examine the religious belief system of ancient Egypt. When the Children of Israel were enslaved in Egypt, they were exposed to over 1,500 deities who were thought to control every aspect of life. Each one of these deities was responsible for different aspects of life on a daily basis. Many of them were directed to some aspect of the afterlife. It was often these gods who were given the most attention, which enables us to understand that people are concerned with what happens when their life in this world comes to an end. If you served these gods faithfully and lived a worthy life, you could be ensured of an existence beyond this world.

Move into more modern-day religions. Those which promote reincarnation teach that each successive life moves a person either up the scale or down, depending on how the previous life was lived. The goal is to live consecutive lives in such a worthy manner that you move progressively up in the order until you reach a point where your existence transcends life in this material world.

For many other religions which actually teach some form of eternal life, the basis for receiving such a life is determined by the life you live here in this world and the works you are able to accomplish. The Vikings were hoping to reach Valhalla, and the only sure way to arrive at the great banquet was to be worthy unto death. For the proponents of Islam, the only absolute assured way to reach paradise is to die in the service of Allah. In many of the religions which resemble Christianity, the basis of maintaining a relationship with the god they believe in is to live in such a way as to be worthy of acceptance. If you live a worthy life, then you will one day be rewarded with the blessings promised. Each one of these religions promises something different, but in the end, all are based on the same premise. In order for a person to be saved and receive eternal life, the individual must accomplish for themselves what is demanded. Failure to do so means exclusion.

In every religious structure throughout history, the one common denominator is that people must earn their own salvation. The forces at work, or whatever god believed in, have laid out the formula for salvation, and it is up to the individual to achieve it. Because this philosophy appeals to the innate nature of human beings, it is captivating to the human heart. If I feel the need to do something and my belief system offers me the opportunity to do the "things" which are needful for salvation, then it meets the felt need I have. If the person is "faithful" to what is required in the religious system, there is a great sense of self-justification and even self-righteousness in the person's life.

Here are several Scripture passages in which God reveals the appeals of false beliefs:

John 5:39 — You search the Scriptures because you think that in them you have eternal life, and it is they that bear witness about me

Jeremiah 8:9 — The wise men shall be put to shame; they shall be dismayed and taken; behold, they have rejected the word of the LORD, so what wisdom is in them?

Matt 22:29 — But Jesus answered them, "You are wrong, because you know neither the Scriptures nor the power of God.

2 Timothy 4:3 For the time is coming when people will not endure sound teaching, but having itching ears they will accumulate for themselves teachers to suit their own passions.

Rom 1:22-23 Claiming to be wise, they became fools, 23 and exchanged the glory of the immortal God for images resembling mortal man and birds and animals and creeping things.

1 Timothy 6:5 And constant friction among people who are depraved in mind and deprived of the truth, imagining that godliness is a means of gain.

2 Tim 3:2-5 For people will be lovers of self, lovers of money, proud, arrogant, abusive, disobedient to their parents, ungrateful, unholy, 3 heartless, unappeasable, slanderous, without self-control, brutal, not loving good, 4 treacherous, reckless, swollen with conceit, lovers of pleasure rather than lovers of God, 5 having the appearance of godliness, but denying its power. Avoid such people.

Eph 4:14   So that we may no longer be children, tossed to and fro by the waves and carried about by every wind of doctrine, by human cunning, by craftiness in deceitful schemes.

Acts 17:16-18   Now, while Paul was waiting for them in Athens, his spirit was provoked within him as he saw that the city was full of idols. 17 So he reasoned in the synagogue with the Jews and the devout persons and in the marketplace every day with those who happened to be there. 18 Some of the Epicurean and Stoic philosophers also conversed with him. And some said, "What does this babbler wish to say?" Others said, "He seems to be a preacher of foreign divinities"--because he was preaching Jesus and the resurrection.

One of the challenges, even among God's people, is that a person can easily move from dependence upon God and His grace to the belief that what they do determines their relationship with God. This was uniquely true among the religious leaders of Jesus' day. The Pharisees and Sadducees structured a belief system in which faithful adherence to the Law of Moses determined God's favor or disapproval. The members of these two groups believed they had achieved a relationship with God through their own efforts, and thus, they were elevated above the common people around them. The self-righteous attitude they embraced moved them to hold all other people in contempt, and it made God unapproachable.

Jesus' words to them are among the harshest in the whole Bible:

> "Woe to you, scribes and Pharisees, hypocrites! For you are like whitewashed tombs, which outwardly appear beautiful, but within are full of dead people's bones and all uncleanness. 28 So you also outwardly appear

righteous to others, but within you are full of hypocrisy and lawlessness." Matthew 23:27-28

Why Man's Search For The "Spiritual" Can Never Give Reconciliation Or Peace

There are many people in the world today who declare they are "spiritual," but they do not believe in God. The view that God is distant and uncaring or harsh and judgmental has moved many people away from traditional Christian beliefs. The fact that people have a desire to be "spiritual" without a relationship with God is evidence that there is a spiritual component to human life.

The human spirit was created for a relationship with God, and in the absence of this true spiritual relationship, each person is left to search for something to fill the void left in their heart. This is a futile endeavor because, without a guide or a means to accomplish a connection with what is truly spiritual, each individual is left to devise their own understanding of what spiritual life is to entail. Scripture speaks of man's endless search for God or the spiritual in many different ways.

Jer 6:14	They have healed the wound of my people lightly, saying, 'Peace, peace,' when there is no peace.
Phil 3:19	Their end is destruction, their god is their belly, and they glory in their shame, with minds set on earthly things.
Jer 23:12	Therefore their way shall be to them like slippery paths in the darkness, into which they shall be driven and fall, for I will bring disaster upon them in the year of their punishment, declares the LORD.

Matt 15:14   Let them alone; they are blind guides. And if the blind lead the blind, both will fall into a pit."

Col 2:8   See to it that no one takes you captive by philosophy and empty deceit, according to human tradition, according to the elemental spirits of the world, and not according to Christ.

Solomon wrote, *"Every man's way is right in his own eyes, But the LORD weighs the hearts"* Proverbs 21:2. Additionally, how can a person ever know if they have achieved what is required to be truly spiritual or a true connection with a spiritual being if each person is to discover what is required by their own understanding? This leaves an individual always questioning if what is being done in connection to their spirituality is true and correct. What if something is missed or if a person fails to accomplish what is believed to be required? How is a person to regain true spirituality or a "right-standing" before God? Try harder! Be more diligent! The list is endless: Sacrifice more, pray more, serve more. There is no possibility of ever having assurance or peace if there is no accepted understanding of a universal truth for all people. How is it possible for a person to know God and His will for their life if we turn from God and seek to find Him by our own efforts? If God is truly God, then He is so far above and beyond us that He is incomprehensible.

God Is Incomprehensible

Moses wrote these words for us:

> *"The secret things belong to the LORD our God, but the things that are revealed belong to us and to our children forever, that we may do all the words of this law."* (Deut. 29:29)

As finite human beings, our ability to "know" is limited. We have the ability to comprehend some of what is contained in this physical world. Creation is wondrous and magnificent to behold, and there are many aspects of our created universe that are being discovered and understood. Humanity will never fully understand everything about creation. But for the sake of argument, if we could exhaust all knowledge of our material existence, what would we still not know? Apart from what God has revealed, we have no knowledge of what lies beyond the grave. We have no understanding of what exactly takes place the moment a person dies, and their spirit is separated from their physical body. In our attempt to deny God, many philosophies and theories have been proposed for the origin of life on this planet. The hypothesis of evolution would teach us that we are an accident of nature. But even this belief system breaks down because no one can answer the question about the origin of matter or how the first microscopic forms of life began. It is all simply guesswork!

Think for a moment about what was present when nothing was present! Take away the galaxies, our own universe, and solar system, remove all created matter, and what are you left with? Before there was anything, and when there was nothing, there was God. God existed and still exists above and beyond all created matter of this material world. If we accept what the Bible reveals about the creation of the world as an act of God, then we must also accept the limitations implied in this Divine action. God created what exists, but God is not bound by what exists. God set in place natural law, but God is not bound by natural law. God brought forth life and is the source of all living things, but God Himself had no beginning, and because He is God, He has no end. Creation itself is limited in the amount of time it can exist; God is limitless being without beginning and without end.

We know and are continually growing in our understanding of what is present for us to explore. But we are bound to the limits of creation itself. Since God exists outside of our material existence, it is impossible for any human being to know God or truly comprehend that which is spiritual. Without God's divine intervention into creation, it would be impossible for any human being to know about God or know God. The intervention of God takes place for each individual at what we understand to be conversion or the working of faith in the life of a human being by the Holy Spirit.

CHAPTER FIVE

WHAT HAPPENS AT CONVERSION

"Every story of conversion is the story of a blessed defeat."

– C. S. Lewis

There are times when our use of language confuses the people we are seeking to engage and even those who would agree with us. We speak of people being converted, and by this, we mean that something has changed in their hearts. So, what does this mean? I do not like oysters on the half shell, but if my friend convinces me to try them with a unique sauce, he says I will enjoy the taste. I try them, and I am converted! I now like to eat oysters.

The word conversion carries the idea that I have experienced something and thus made a decision that has moved me to change my previous opinion or understanding. While Christian conversion can be understood the right way, the use of this term has its limitations. In His discussion with Nicodemus, Jesus chose to use the phrase "born again." This phrase also has its limitations, as is seen in John 3 when Nicodemus asks if it is possible for a man to enter into his mother's womb and be born a second time. Jesus then directs his attention to the work of the Spirit of God. Using the wind, as an illustration, Jesus asks if Nicodemus can understand the wind? Can you tell where it comes from or where it is going? The Spirit of God is present, but you can only tell He is present by what He does. In the same way, you can feel the breeze, and you can see the working of the Spirit in a person's life. Paul gives us an understanding of this when he instructs the church in Ephesus on exactly what happens when a person becomes a Christian. According to Paul, the grace of God is at work offering to a person the ability to have Jesus as Savior. The Spirit is at work to join with the human spirit and enable the person to have faith. Faith then holds onto the truth of what Jesus accomplished through His life, death, and resurrection. The moment faith is created, the human spirit is joined with and united to the Spirit of God who dwells within all believers (Ephesians 2:8-9).

The Spirit of God dwelling in union with the human spirit constitutes what we understand to be converted or to be born again. The person who experiences this working of God in their life has, in that instant, become a child of God and thus an heir of heaven. There is nothing the person has to do. There are no rubrics to follow. There is no list of rules which are now applied to the person's life, and there are no conditions placed upon the person to be worthy of the "gift" which has been given. If we want to speak in terms of the truth, all human beings are unworthy of knowing or being in a relationship with God. He is holy, and we are sinful. He is righteous, and we are dirty and unclean. He is totally beyond our ability to understand or grasp, yet He is the one who chooses to reveal Himself to us so that we might be blessed by Him. Jesus was born into this world to open the way for every person to know God as a loving Father who desires to forgive them and bless them throughout their earthly life and then bestow on them eternal life.

It is also important to note that this action of God to enable a person to be born again is not absolute! God does not force conversion upon a person. It is an amazing truth about God that His love is limitless, even to the point that He would risk losing us rather than force us to love Him in return. The theological term we use for this is "free will." God gave our first parents the ability to choose to love Him and live in a relationship with Him, as well as the ability to choose for themselves to walk away from Him. Sadly, we know what they did.

The free will of all humanity is now itself corrupted by sin. The fall was total and complete, leaving every human heart yearning for the spiritual but unable to truly grasp it. There was absolutely no way for any person to return to God. In our fallen state, we do not truly want a God Who is holy and wholly other than us. We are content with our counterfeits which offer us solace and the opportunity to satisfy our own spiritual yearnings. The miracle of God's grace is that when we rejected Him as our God, He never rejected us. Instead, He set in motion the prophetic history leading to Christ and then to the coming of the Holy Spirit on the day of Pentecost. It is God's limitless love that is at work when the Spirit comes to a person to create faith by which the spirit of the person can know Jesus as the one who has forgiven them and through Him be adopted as a child of God. The option is still present for a person to reject the offer of forgiveness, but if a person is born again, it is because the Spirit of God has enabled this to happen. This is why the text of John 3 more literally says, we are born "from above."

In proper theological terms, this dynamic is called the *Crux Theologorum,* or the cross of theology, or the cross of the theologian. It is explained as follows: if a person is saved, it is through the working of God. The Holy Spirit is the one who has worked to create faith in Jesus as Savior. If, however, a person is lost, it is the result of their own action or choice. If salvation is the reality of a person's life, then it has been the work of God from beginning to end. From the prophetic promises to the coming of Jesus and all the way to the point that the Spirit of God enables a person to have faith in Jesus, salvation is totally the working of God.

By contrast, there are many in modern-day Christianity who have rejected this understanding of free will and the inability of a human being to have faith apart from the working of God. There is the belief on the part of some that God has accomplished salvation through the work of Christ on the cross, and He now offers forgiveness freely to the people of this world. It is now up to each individual to choose for themselves if they reject or accept Jesus as their Savior. This understanding negates the understanding of absolute grace and places the person once again in the driver's seat with regard to their eternal salvation. Another way to say this is that God has done His part; now, you must do your part. This theological bent became very popular in early America due to the mindset that a person must forge their own way and build a new life, carving it out of the rugged frontier. "Pull yourself up by your bootstraps" is the way we generally hear it said. This means you are responsible for every aspect of your own life. Either you do it, or it won't get done. This belief verges on what we have addressed previously in that as fallen human beings, we create a god who is according to our own understanding, and we determine the rules by which we approach and engage in a relationship with

Him. If we are in control, then God is subject to us and not the other way around.

Once conversion or the new birth from above takes place, there will be a new way of life for the person who is now a child of God. This new life includes the indwelling of the Spirit of God, living in connection and communion with a person's spirit. This is the fulfillment of all the "temple" imagery in the Bible. Where God once dwelt in the temple in Jerusalem, He now dwells in the literal bodies of every believer.

This communion between the Holy Spirit of God and a person's spirit opens the way for each child of God to instantly know God's perfect will for their lives. God the Spirit, who is one with the Father and the Son, is now dwelling in union and communion with the human spirit, and He is communicating God's perfect will directly to the person. Paul speaks of this in 1 Corinthians 2:11 when he writes, *"For who among people knows the thoughts of a person except the spirit of the person that is in him? So also, the thoughts of God no one knows, except the Spirit of God."* And again, in Romans 8:26, *"Likewise the Spirit helps us in our weakness. For we do not know what to pray for as we ought, but the Spirit himself intercedes for us with groanings too deep for words."* The Spirit of God dwelling in union with the human spirit is communicating the heart of God for a person's life directly from the Father to His child, and the desires and concerns of this same child directly back to the Father.

It is ironic that the ancient philosophers understood this Trichotomy of man when they gave us an illustration concerning how to strengthen our life in this world to live in an upright way. The use of the chariot pulled by two horses was a common image of the struggle raging within the human heart. The story is told this way:

A chariot is being pulled by two horses along a narrow path with a steep embankment on one side and a deep canyon on the other. The horse on the inside represents the spirit of a man. This horse is pulling against the second horse, which is the flesh of a man. The spirit horse struggles to keep the chariot on the path and running directly down the path. The horse of the flesh desires to pull the chariot into the canyon to utter destruction. In the middle, the one driving the chariot is the soul of a man. The soul is the battleground for a person's life, and the horse which will win the struggle between life and death is the horse you feed the most.

It is also interesting that in American Indian lore, the same story is told but with a unique twist. It is told by the Cherokee as follows:

Once, an old man and his grandson were walking through the woods when the grandfather turned to the young man and said, "Young one, inside all of us, there is a battle raging between two wolves. You have felt it even in your young years, and I have felt it all my life. One of the wolves is evil – he is anger, envy, greed, regret, arrogance, resentment, lies, hatred, and ego. The other is good – he is love, joy, peace, hope, humility, kindness, empathy, generosity, compassion, truth, and faith. Everyone has this battle going on inside them."

> They walked a little further in silence until the young boy stopped and asked, "Grandfather, which wolf will win?"
> The wise old man simply replied, "The one you feed."

The indwelling of the Spirit of God provides the way for the child of God to grow in faith and love. The maturity to become a clear reflection of the heart of the Father in the world is living inside each one of us. The key will always be that we listen to and feed into our lives the things which strengthen our relationship with the Spirit of God. These would include worship, the study of Scripture, fellowship with other believers, and a life lived in devotion to God. To fail to do the things which keep faith and connection to the Spirit strong results in a life lived being controlled by the passions of the flesh. If we feed the flesh and not the spirit, our lives will reflect the carnal nature of the people of this world.

CHAPTER SIX

HOW DO WE LIVE IN OUR NEW RELATIONSHIP WITH GOD AS ONE WHO IS RE-BORN?

We may not preach a crucified Savior without being also crucified men and women. It is not enough to wear an ornamental cross as a pretty decoration. The cross that Paul speaks about was burned into his very flesh, was branded into his being, and only the Holy Spirit can burn the true cross into our innermost life.

— *A. B. Simpson*

With the new birth comes a new understanding of life itself. When we take the time to truly look at the people of our broken world, most of them are living aimlessly. They are striving for significance through either work or money. When the physical body begins to show signs of age, there are numerous surgeries that can be performed to enhance the physical appearance and remove the effects of aging. People are searching for something or someone to give them meaning and purpose. Sadly, many will never find it because they are looking in the wrong direction. People think this world offers all the answers to the meaning of life. More money, a bigger home, a new spouse, a career move, a retirement account, and so many more "things" bring satisfaction for a moment, but it does not last.

There is at the core of every person one great desire. We want to be wanted. We yearn for someone to accept us and love us unconditionally, regardless of how badly we have messed up in the past or how much of a screw-up we are today. No amount of worldly goods can satisfy the desires of the human heart. No relationship with another person can fully complete us without also having a relationship with God. It is true we were created for relationship. In Genesis 2, God said to Himself, "It is not good for man to be alone, I will make a helper for him." Creation was "good," as God had declared it, but it was not yet fully perfect. Not perfect in the sense of lacking in holiness, but not perfect in the sense of not yet complete. God is Trinity, and as such, He dwells in relationship with Himself, Father, Son, and Spirit. If we are truly created in the image of God, then we are created for relationships. Relationship with God and with one another.

Only when we understand and live in our relationship with God can we truly understand and value our relationships with other people. Using the relationship of marriage as an example, if a person goes into a marriage seeking to find fulfillment, disappointment awaits. This places a great burden on the spouse which is impossible to fulfill. The end result is that one spouse, or both, becomes disillusioned in the marriage, and divorce happens. The reason for this is that the one spouse enters the relationship seeking what they believe will lead to contentment in life. Marriage was never intended to be focused on what a person receives, but rather on what a person gives to bless the other spouse. It is about giving and not receiving. Paul said in

Ephesians 5, *"a husband is to love his wife as Christ loved the church and gave Himself up for her."* When the focus is on sacrifice and not reward, then there is joy in giving blessings to the other person. This is the heart of God!

When Jesus went to the cross, He was sacrificing everything, 100% of who He was, unto death. At that exact moment, He was receiving nothing, 0%, in return. Yes, He was receiving judgment! He was receiving damnation. He was rejected by all humanity and judged by God as an unworthy sinner as He hung upon the cross. He was giving all He was to bless us! At that moment, He received nothing in return, but when His sacrifice was complete, Jesus received everything. He was glorified by the Father, and every person who is brought to faith in Him is a reward that brings joy to His heart. Understand that it is not about us! It is not about what we do. It is always about God and His great love for us.

Years ago, in the deep Southern part of the United States, the phrase "born again" was never used. There was a phrase that has fallen into disuse but captures the understanding of God's love for a person. When a person was born again or converted, the people would say, "they were seized by a Great Affection." The Great Affection was the great love of God which has overwhelmed them and revealed to them the depths of God's limitless love. When this Great Affection took hold of a person, their life was changed. It was changed in response to having been loved so deeply.

What does it mean to live as a Christian? What is required of us and the people of God in this world? Absolutely nothing! For something to be required is to be placed under the law, and therefore we would be subject to consequences for failing to keep the law. We are a people under grace, God's limitless love! So, answer the question, "Do you have to go to church to be a Christian?" Many would sadly say yes to this question and thus place a burden on the backs of God's children. What is it which determines heaven or hell? What is necessary for a person to be saved? The only thing necessary for a person to be assured of eternal life with God is faith in Jesus as Savior. And even the faith born in our hearts is given to us as a gift of His grace. You do not have to go to church to be a Christian. The fact that you are a Christian means you get to go to church. Our life is not to be lived believing we are to obtain God's favor by what we do. We are to live a life of response to the grace of God we have received and freely choose to do what honors Him in our lives.

Created In The Image Of God

As you can see, being created in the image of God far extends the simple definition of being originally created in a state of holiness and righteousness. It means that God created us to be a reflection of Him and His nature. As triune beings, there are aspects to human beings which enable us to live in relationship with God and with each other, which far transcends the superficial level to which so many people have become accustomed.

There is in the very design of every human being the ability to dwell in a union and fellowship with God in which God unites Himself, His Spirit, with each of us, our human spirit. This union provides the opportunity for God to communicate and live in a relationship with each person on an intimate level. This relationship has been explained by many people in various ways. As I have stated, some use the Biblical terminology found in John chapter 3, calling it "born again." Others have grasped onto the phrase "conversion." Within the context of historical Christianity, the understanding of the Spirit's indwelling at the moment of baptism marked the beginning of this new relationship. Today the historical understanding of Baptism has been set aside and a new understanding has become the accepted view.

The understanding within modern Christianity is that God has created us to live in an intimate relationship with Himself, and He has provided the means by which this relationship is established and maintained. This is understood to be the indwelling of His Spirit and the continual spiritual growth of the Christian through the Word of God, which is guided by the Spirit dwelling within. While this is true, when we as modern-day Christians set aside what the church has taught for two thousand years, we prove ourselves arrogant. God has revealed throughout the Scriptures that He is a God who works through "means."

The Gospel is the "means" by which God chose to save all humanity from sin and the consequences which sin brought upon every human being. This said the Gospel must be properly understood! The Gospel of Jesus Christ is, first and foremost, a historical event. Jesus was actually born into this world through the working of God in the virgin Mary. He was fully and completely God who became fully and completely human. Jesus was in every way just as we are, with the exception of sin, (Hebrews 4:15). He was born holy and remained holy throughout His entire earthly life. Having grown to manhood, Jesus did all which the New Testament Gospel writings reveal. He preached, taught, healed the sick, raised the dead, performed many miracles, and then He was arrested, suffered, and died on the cross. Jesus was raised on the third day, never to die again. He ascended into heaven from where He will one day return for the final judgment. These are actual historical events. This is the historical Gospel!

The preaching or proclamation of the Gospel is the "means" by which the historical events Jesus accomplished impact an individual's life. The New Testament bears out the truth that preaching the Gospel of Jesus Christ is the avenue (means) by which the Holy Spirit of God enters into union with an individual's spirit and creates faith. We generally speak of faith dwelling in the "heart" of a person. While this is the phrase we use, it is a shorthand way of speaking to what is a much deeper connection.

Ephesians 2:8 speaks of the working of faith as a gift given to us by God by which we are enabled to believe in Jesus as our Savior. *"For by grace you have been saved through faith. And this is not your own doing; it is the gift of God."* Jesus speaks clearly of the necessity of faith in the sense of believing as the means by which a person is saved - *"Whoever believes in the Son has eternal life; whoever does not obey the Son shall not see life, but the wrath of God remains on him"* (John 3:36). In this passage, believing is more than simply understanding the facts, but it is believing in the sense of having faith in Jesus as your Savior.

The apostle Paul writes to the church in Rome of the necessity of having someone proclaim the message of Jesus and His cross for the purpose of salvation. *"How then will they call on him in whom they have not believed? And how are they to believe in him of whom they have never heard? And how are they to hear without someone preaching?"* (Romans 10:14). And again, *"So faith comes from hearing, and hearing through the word of Christ"* (Romans 10:17). To know of the historical events concerning the history of Jesus' life, death, and resurrection will not save a person. It is only when the Gospel is proclaimed, and the Holy Spirit works faith in the heart of a person that conversion takes place. Conversion is that moment when the unbeliever becomes a believer!

This is what God proclaimed He would do through the prophet Ezekiel,

> *"And I will give you a new heart, and a new spirit I will put within you. And I will remove the heart of stone from your flesh and give you a heart of flesh."* (Ezekiel 36:26)

What happens when a person experiences conversion has nothing to do with the physical part of the body, what we call the heart. The heart is part of the **soma** or body, and as such, it functions and serves its purpose to keep the physical body alive. In a much more technical sense, conversion is the moment when the spirit of a human being is brought into a relationship with the Holy Spirit of God.

The lives of the Old Testament people of God focused on the city of Jerusalem and the Temple. When Solomon dedicated the Temple, the glory of God descended upon him and entered the temple. So great was the presence of God that the priests who were ministering at the dedication ceremony could not remain in the temple but had to exit and stand among the people outside.

> 2 Chronicles 7:1-3 *As soon as Solomon finished his prayer, fire came down from heaven and consumed the burnt offering and the sacrifices, and the glory of the LORD filled the temple. 2 And the priests could not enter the house of the LORD, because the glory of the LORD filled the LORD's house. 3 When all the people of Israel saw the fire come down and the glory of the LORD on the temple, they bowed down with their faces to the ground on the pavement and worshiped and gave thanks to the LORD, saying, "For he is good, for his steadfast love endures forever."*

The people of Israel understood that God dwelt in the city of Jerusalem, in the temple. He dwelt in the holy of holies on the mercy seat between the outstretched wings of the cherubim on the Ark of the Covenant. If you wanted to worship God, you must travel to the temple, for this was the place where God dwelt in the midst of His people. At the time of the exile to Babylon, Daniel faced West toward Jerusalem when he would bow down and pray. Jews all over the world would pray toward Jerusalem, not the heavens, when they prayed, for they were praying to God, and He was present in the temple. When the news of the destruction of the Temple in 586BC spread around the world, the Jews were in despair. If there is no temple in Jerusalem, there is no God in Israel!

God has promised to do something new, and through Jesus, He has opened the way to dwell intimately in connection and fellowship with every single person who believes. The apostle Paul goes to great lengths to explain this to the Church of his day. *"Or do you not know that your body is a temple of the Holy Spirit within you, whom you have from God? You are not your own"* (1 Corinthians 6:19). And *"By the Holy Spirit who dwells within us, guard the good deposit entrusted to you"* (2 Timothy 1:14). It is clear from the New Testament that the Holy Spirit dwells in each believer, but in what way?

The Holy Spirit has entered into each believer, and we are now considered the temple of God, the place where God dwells. The Holy Spirit, who is a person of the Trinity, is now in union and fellowship with the Father and the Son and also with each believer. He is present, indwelling each believer, for the purpose of connecting us through faith in Christ with the Father who desires to have us as His Children. The Spirit is the One through whom our relationship is established and remains strong. Paul writes: *"Likewise the Spirit helps us in our weakness. For we do not know what to pray for as we ought, but the Spirit himself intercedes for us with groanings too deep for words. And he who searches hearts knows what is the mind of the Spirit, because the Spirit intercedes for the saints according to the will of God."* (Romans 8:26-27). The Spirit has actually joined Himself to the human spirit for the purpose of establishing this new relationship. This is rebirth or to be born again.

The image of the Temple is once again pictured in the writings of the Apostle Peter when he writes: *"As you come to him, a living stone rejected by men but in the sight of God chosen and precious, you yourselves like living stones are being built up as a spiritual house, to be a holy priesthood, to offer spiritual sacrifices acceptable to God through Jesus Christ"* (1 Peter 2:4-5). The temple was built out of lifeless stones! We were each lifeless apart from the working of God, the Spirit, and the gift of faith. We are now living stones brought together and connected, stone upon stone, to become the temple of the living God. Not a building, but each individual Christian connected to one another and together becoming the New Testament Temple, or the Church, the place where God dwells in the midst of His people. All of this happens when the Gospel proclamation is made, and the Spirit of God works faith in a human heart.

As it was stated earlier, God has chosen to work through means. The Gospel of Jesus Christ is a historical fact. Jesus lived, died, and rose for the whole world's salvation. The proclamation of the Gospel, the message of salvation through faith in Him, is the means by which what was accomplished on the cross is applied to the life of an individual so that union and fellowship with God can be restored. The preaching of the Gospel is one of the means or avenues by which God the Holy Spirit works to reconcile a lost sinner to our loving God.

CHAPTER SEVEN

TO BE A CHOSEN PEOPLE

"There's no greater courage and strength that compares to knowing you are loved."

– Koki Oyuke

God has also revealed that He works in the life of a person through Baptism and the Lord's Supper. While this is not intended to be a theological dissertation on the sacraments of the church, we would be remiss if we did not address some basic foundational truths God reveals in His Word.

In the Church, there are two distinct ways in which baptism is understood. One is that it is an "ordinance" by which an individual who has responded to the Gospel proclamation is to affirm and profess publicly their own personal commitment and devotion to God. This understanding places the action of baptism squarely upon the shoulders of the one being baptized.

The other, more historical understanding of baptism, does the exact opposite. Instead of baptism being the action of an individual, the

Church has historically understood baptism to be the working of God to save sinful people and restore them as His children. To fully understand this, it is necessary to examine baptism in light of its predecessor in the Old Testament, namely circumcision.

When God chose Abraham to be the father of His people, God established a covenant, and this covenant was given a "sign" by which the people of God entered into and lived as God's people. The sign of the covenant was circumcision.

> *This is my covenant, which you shall keep, between me and you and your offspring after you: Every male among you shall be circumcised. You shall be circumcised in the flesh of your foreskins, and it shall be a sign of the covenant between me and you. He who is eight days old among you shall be circumcised. Every male throughout your generations, whether born in your house or bought with your money from any foreigner who is not of your offspring, both he who is born in your house and he who is bought with your money, shall surely be circumcised. So shall my covenant be in your flesh an everlasting covenant. Any uncircumcised male who is not circumcised in the flesh of his foreskin shall be cut off from his people; he has broken my covenant"* (Genesis 17:10-14).

Now understand what God said to Abraham. He and his descendants were to take every male child and perform a circumcision on the eighth day of their life. If an individual came into their midst who was older, this act of circumcision was to be performed on that person, but under normal circumstances, it was performed at eight days old. This child had no say in this being done. It was commanded by God to be done by those who were His covenant people. If the foreskin was removed, the child circumcised was included in the covenant people. If the circumcision did not take place, then the child was "cut off" from the covenant. There is definitely a play on words in the text. Cut off the foreskin, or the child is cut off!

It is the Apostle Paul who makes the direct tie between circumcision as the entry point into the old covenant and baptism as the entry point into the new covenant established by Jesus.

> *"In him also you were circumcised with a circumcision made without hands, by putting off the body of the flesh, by the circumcision of Christ, having been buried with him in baptism, in which you were also raised with him through faith in the powerful working of God, who raised him from the dead"* (Colossians 2:11-12).

Paul declares to us that it is baptism through which a person is connected to Jesus and by which this individual receives the benefits of what Jesus accomplished on the cross for him. There are a multitude of Scripture passages that affirm that the forgiveness of sin accomplished on the cross is given to an individual at the moment of Baptism because it is in the act of Baptism that a person becomes part of the covenant people of God.

> *"And Peter said to them, "Repent and be baptized every one of you in the name of Jesus Christ for the forgiveness of your sins, and you will receive the gift of the Holy Spirit."*
> Acts 2:38

> *"But when the goodness and loving kindness of God our Savior appeared, he saved us, not because of works done by*

us in righteousness, but according to his own mercy, by the washing of regeneration and renewal of the Holy Spirit." Titus 3:4-5

"Jesus answered, "Truly, truly, I say to you, unless one is born of water and the Spirit, he cannot enter the kingdom of God." John 3:5

The foundational understanding of Scripture is that only God can forgive sins. We hear multiple times in the Bible that the forgiveness of sins and the working of the Holy Spirit are intimately tied to the act of Baptism. If the Spirit is working and forgiveness is being granted, then it is God who is working in the life of an individual. Therefore, Baptism is a means by which what Jesus accomplished on Calvary's cross is applied to the life of an individual who stands in need of forgiveness.

There is one more aspect of God working in the life of a person, which needs to be understood if we are going to find our comfort and assurance in Him. Faith itself is a gift of God which is clearly stated by Paul in Ephesians 2:8. But what is faith? Is faith the ability of a person to intellectually comprehend who Jesus is and what He accomplished on the cross for the whole world? The answer to this is no! Faith is not something the Holy Spirit works in our mind, but something which is created in the "heart" or, more precisely, in the "spirit" of a person. It is because faith is not an intellectual exercise but the working of God within the spirit of a person that faith is not dependent upon the age of an individual. If faith required intellectual ascent, then those who are severely mentally handicapped, the extremely young, or even someone who has experienced brain trauma could not be saved and would perish forever. Paul, the Old Testament scholar that he was, says in 1Timothy 2:4 that God wants *"all people to be saved."*

Another aspect of Baptism that should not be overlooked is the fact that if circumcision was the precursor or foreshadowing in the Old Testament of what baptism would be in the New Testament, then it is true that the fulfillment is greater than the act which foreshadowed it. The act of circumcision was limited in that only the male members of the Old Testament people could bear the sign. Women were not excluded from the covenant, but they were unable to bear in their bodies the visible sign of the covenant. What was foreshadowed finds a greater expression in the fulfillment when Baptism is given. Now, both males and females are bearers of the sign of the covenant. Both receive the gift of God in baptism and live with the reality that they bear the name of God upon them, which was imprinted as the water was poured and the words were spoken.

While circumcision was given to the people of God as both the entry point into the covenant and the sign which they bore as belonging to God, there was also a meal of celebration or a covenant meal. This covenant meal or meal of relationship was foreshadowed in the first Passover meal and fully realized in the Upper Room when Jesus took what was of the meal and transformed the meaning into something greater. However, the full realization of what the meal means was shown to us when God established the covenant with His people at Mt. Sinai. Because this is such a vital part of our life with God, I want to take a moment to understand what God was doing then and what we have received today from Him.

When Jesus gathered with the disciples on the final Passover evening, He did something during the meal which had not been done before. Now understand, this meal had been celebrated by these twelve men with Him every year of their lives. It was a scripted meal with different foods eaten at specific times along with the words which were given by

Moses for them to recite concerning the meaning of each thing they ate. Yet Jesus breaks tradition and interjects something new into the meal, which the apostles understood was for them to carry on into the future of the Church.

Jesus said:

> *"While they were eating, He took some bread, and after a blessing He broke it, and gave it to them, and said, "Take it; this is My body." And when He had taken a cup and given thanks, He gave it to them, and they all drank from it. And He said to them, "This is My blood of the covenant, which is poured out for many"* (Mk. 14:22-24).

> *"And in the same way He took the cup after they had eaten, saying, "This cup which is poured out for you is the new covenant in My blood"* (Lk. 22:20).

> *"And when He had taken a cup and given thanks, He gave it to them, saying, "Drink from it, all of you; for this is My blood of the covenant, which is poured out for many for forgiveness of sin"* (Matt. 26:27-28).

In each of these accounts, Jesus draws attention to the cup, which is His blood that is poured out and given. It is the blood of the covenant. What covenant is Jesus addressing? Passover was not the establishment of a covenant between God and His people. Circumcision was given as a sign of the covenant, not the establishment of the covenant. Is it the covenant of the Law given on Mt. Sinai? The only problem with this was that the Law was not given as a covenant. The Law was given to show the people how they should live as the covenant people of

God. So what covenant is Jesus referring to when He takes from the Passover meal and does something new?

The Covenant With Israel

To understand this, we have to go back to the account of the Exodus and the events which took place at Mt. Sinai. Generally, when we recall the events of the Exodus, we remember the plagues, the parting of the Red Sea, traveling to Mt. Sinai, and the giving of the Ten Commandments. All these events happened just as Moses recorded them. The only problem is that we recall the "big" events and omit the most important one because it doesn't seem to stand out like the others.

It all took place in Exodus 24. Please take some time to read the following text and seek to grasp its significance.

> *"Then He said to Moses, "Come up to the LORD, you and Aaron, Nadab and Abihu, and seventy of the elders of Israel, and you shall worship at a distance. Moses alone, however, shall approach the LORD, but they shall not approach, nor shall the people come up with him." Then Moses came and reported to the people all the words of the LORD and all the ordinances; and all the people answered with one voice and said, "All the words which the LORD has spoken we will do!" And Moses wrote down all the words of the LORD. Then he got up early in the morning, and built an altar at the foot of the mountain with twelve memorial stones for the twelve tribes of Israel. And he sent young men of the sons of Israel, and they offered burnt offerings and sacrificed bulls as peace offerings to the LORD. Moses took*

half of the blood and put it in basins, and the other half of the blood he sprinkled on the altar. Then he took the Book of the Covenant and read it as the people listened; and they said, "All that the LORD has spoken we will do, and we will be obedient!" So Moses took the blood and sprinkled it on the people, and said, "Behold the blood of the covenant, which the LORD has made with you in accordance with all these words." Then Moses went up with Aaron, Nadab and Abihu, and seventy of the elders of Israel, and they saw the God of Israel; and under His feet there appeared to be a pavement of sapphire, as clear as the sky itself. Yet He did not reach out with His hand against the nobles of the sons of Israel; and they saw God, and they ate and drank" (Exodus 24 1-11).

As I said, the giving of the Law revealed what God desired of His people as they lived in a relationship with Him. When Moses ascended the mountain, he received the full accounting of the Law from God. This is not the account of the giving of the Ten Commandments. The text says, *"Then Moses came and reported to the people all the words of the LORD and all the ordinances."* Moses speaks to the people all God has spoken to Him. The response of the people was to voice their commitment to be who God was calling them to be. The people said, *"and all the people answered with one voice and said, "All the words which the LORD has spoken we will do!"*

Because every truth must be established by two witnesses, Moses then writes down all the words he has just spoken to the people, and once they are written, he reads them aloud for all the people to hear.

While Moses is writing down all the words of the Lord, we presume this later became the book of Deuteronomy; the people were building an altar and preparing the sacrifices. When all was made ready, this is what took place: *Then he took the Book of the Covenant and read it as the people listened; and they said, "All that the LORD has spoken we will do, and we will be obedient!"* A second hearing of the words of the covenant and a second affirmation from the people that they do want to be in this covenant with God.

Once the covenant was affirmed twice, Moses established the covenant. The reading of the Law outlined the covenant but did not establish it. There can be no covenant without the shedding of blood. This is evidenced when God made a covenant with Abraham and here on the mountain when it was established with all of Israel.

Abraham's covenant has ties to what Jesus did on the night of the Passover and at the cross. While the covenant established on Mt. Sinai was entered into with the people affirming their desire to be faithful to God in all things. The covenant with Abraham was one in which God chose Abraham to be the father of the people of God and the one through whom the Messiah would come. Because this was God's total choice and action Abraham does not pledge his faithfulness to it. It is not that he is unwilling, but God chooses to pledge Himself solely to the fulfillment of His promises.

The Covenant With Abraham

In the ancient world, when a covenant was established between two individuals, it was made binding by the shedding of blood. As we see in the following text, the animals of the sacrifice were split in two, the pieces laid out, and once prepared, the two individuals entering into the covenant walked together through the separated pieces of the sacrificial animals. The pledge each of them was making was that if either one of them violated the covenant, one was to be split in two just as the sacrificial animals had been! We would consider this a two-way or bilateral covenant. Both make pledges, both pass through the animals, and both are bound to keep the promises made.

Look at the following account of God's covenant with Abraham and note what is different. God does something unique, which ultimately points us to Christ.

> *And He said to him, "I am the LORD who brought you out of Ur of the Chaldeans, to give you this land to possess it." But he said, "Lord GOD, how may I know that I will possess it?" So He said to him, "Bring Me a three-year-old heifer, a three-year-old female goat, a three-year-old ram, a turtledove, and a young pigeon."* **Then he brought all these to Him and cut them in two, and laid each half opposite the other;** *but he did not cut the birds. 11 And birds of prey came down upon the carcasses, and Abram drove them away. Now when the sun was going down, a deep sleep fell upon Abram; and behold, terror and great darkness fell upon him. Then God said to Abram, "Know for certain that your descendants will be strangers in a land that is not theirs, where they will be enslaved and oppressed for four hundred years. But I will also judge the nation whom they will serve, and afterward they will come out with many possessions. As for you, you shall go to your fathers in peace; you will be buried at a good old age. Then in the fourth generation they will return here, for the wrongdoing of the Amorite is not yet complete."* **Now it came about, when the sun had set, that it was very dark, and behold, a smoking oven and a flaming torch appeared which**

passed between these pieces. On that day the LORD made a covenant with Abram, saying, "To your descendants I have given this land, From the river of Egypt as far as the great river, the river Euphrates: the land of the Kenite, the Kenizzite, the Kadmonite, the Hittite, the Perizzite, the Rephaim, the Amorite, the Canaanite, the Girgashite, and the Jebusite." (Genesis 15:7–21)

Abraham did not pass through the pieces of sacrificed animals; only God did. This covenant was made by God and was based solely on God's promises and God's actions. God would bless Abraham, make his descendants great, give him the land, and through him would come the Messiah. All the promises made were committed to by God alone. God was pledging His faithfulness to Abraham to the point that God would be destroyed if He were to fail to fulfill the promises He had made. This was a one-way or unilateral covenant. This was a covenant of pure grace. God was going to bless regardless of what Abraham did or didn't do.

Return To Mt. Sinai And The Covenant With Israel

Once Moses had written down the words of the covenant and the sacrifices were prepared, Moses established the covenant. *So Moses took the blood and sprinkled it on the people and said, "Behold the blood of the covenant, which the LORD has made with you in accordance with all these words."* Raindrops of blood fall down upon the people. The blood of the covenant applied to them so that the covenant might be established and that the people might be assured of who they were as the people of God.

The covenant having been established with the two hearings of the Law and the two affirmations, and now the sprinkling of the blood, something unique in all the recorded history of God's people is revealed. Where before in the text it is said that everyone was to stay at a distance and only Moses could approach the Lord, now because the covenant has been established through the blood, God invites the leaders to approach Him. *"Then Moses went up with Aaron, Nadab and Abihu, and seventy of the elders of Israel, and they saw the God of Israel; and under His feet there appeared to be a pavement of sapphire, as clear as the sky itself. Yet He did not reach out with His hand against the nobles of the sons of Israel; and they saw God, and they ate and drank."*

God reveals Himself in all of His glorious splendor. He stands as one Who has taken a human form to meet with them, which is evidenced by the fact that the text references His feet and his hand. But what is important for us to understand is that once they have met face to face with God, there is a covenant meal! Once they had seen God in all of His glory revealed in some type of human form, it says, *and they saw God, and they ate and drank"*

The accounts given of when covenants are established are very detailed and exact. Even the account of the upper room and the establishment of the Lord's Supper are given to us four times in Matthew, Mark, Luke, and 1 Corinthians. Details were important. So, where did Moses, Aaron, Nadab, Abihu, and the 70 elders of Israel get the food to eat? They were not told to bring any provisions with them as they ascended the mountain. God gave them the covenant meal to eat. He provided what was needed, and He oversaw all that was done during the meal so that His people might be blessed.

When Jesus sat with His disciples in the upper room and took the bread and wine, speaking of His body and His blood, it was just as on the mountain. God was providing a covenant meal to His people.

He provided what was needed for the meal, and He was with them, overseeing the meal to ensure that His covenant people were blessed.

The New Covenant, which has been established through the blood Jesus shed upon the cross, has been given to us. The blood of the covenant has been applied to us, *For if the blood of goats and bulls and the ashes of a heifer sprinkling those who have been defiled sanctify for the cleansing of the flesh, how much more will the blood of Christ, who through the eternal Spirit offered Himself without blemish to God, cleanse your conscience from dead works to serve the living God?* (Hebrews 9:13-14).

The blood shed and applied, the meal is entered into as a celebration of the reality that we live as the people of God. If we understand the words given by Jesus in some unique and supernaturally spiritual way, He is present in the Lord's Supper. The bread is His body! The wine is His blood! Theologians have argued the meaning long before we picked up the Bible to read it for ourselves. Can we not simply take the words of Jesus as He has given them to us? Do we have to explain every little nuance and all the unknown differences that divide us as God's people? Jesus is present in some way overseeing the meal to ensure that each one who receives it is blessed because that individual is living in a covenant established by the shedding of Jesus' blood upon the cross.

God has made this covenant for us and established it by the blood of His one and only Son. It is a covenant of grace through which we are the ones blessed to be granted forgiveness and eternal life. One day, when our journey in this life draws to a close, we will see God. We will see Him in all of His glorious splendor. The description given in Exodus 24 will be vivid before our eyes. On that day, He will not lift His hand against us! There will be no sin and thus no judgment. There will be acceptance and celebration! And just as we see on Mt. Sinai, all that is needed for our covenant meal is provided for us, and our God sits at the head of the table, as it were, ensuring that we are the ones who receive the full measure of His blessings for all eternity.

CHAPTER EIGHT

CREATION OF MAN AND WOMAN OPPOSITES BUT COMPLETE IN EACH OTHER

"So God created man in His own image, in the image of God He created him; male and female He created them."

– Genesis 1:27

Adam was created in the image of God, and Eve was created from Adam to be his companion! Some have used the order of creation to teach a sharp distinction in authority. Man was created first and therefore has greater authority than woman. To bolster this claim, Paul's first letter to Timothy is used to place women in an inferior state to men; *"I do not permit a woman to teach or to exercise authority over a man; rather, she is to remain quiet. For Adam was formed first, then Eve"* (2:12-13). This passage, in conjunction with 1 Corinthians 11, has seemingly defined the role of women in relation to men. Unfortunately, many times what is stated in Scripture is taken out of the original context and thus the original meaning is skewed.

It is true that Adam was created first and then Eve. There is an "order of creation," but this does not place women in an inferior position to men. Paul makes this clear when he states, *"Nevertheless, in the Lord woman is not independent of man nor man of woman; for as woman was made from man, so man is now born of woman. And all things are from God."* (1 Corinthians 11:11-12). Scripture is clear when roles of responsibility and service are defined, but this has no bearing on the value of an individual as he or she stands before God. The danger is present when we define the worth of a person based on the service a person is called upon by God to perform. The more prominent the role, the more important the person. This attitude nullifies the Gospel of grace and places all people under the burden of works righteousness. What we do does not determine who we are! We gain no value or credit before God through the works of our hands. We are His children by grace and the blood Jesus shed upon the cross and for no other reason. What we do in service to God and to one another flows out of who we are, not the other way around.

When we step back and look at the creation of the man and woman, we see in Scripture they are created equal before God but different. In the differences, we see the image of God clearly revealed. This image is not seen in authority and structure but in intimacy and relationship. Man was created in the image of God, which is visible in his strength and his role as protector and provider. This is not to say that women are not strong. It is not a measurement of simple physical ability, but we do admit, generally speaking, that men are physically stronger than women. Men are created with an innate ability to stand strong and endure the challenges of life and provide security for their families. The man's traditional role as the provider is not simply a societal or cultural stereotype. God created men to stand in this role in relation to women. This has nothing to do with a woman being a stay-at-home mom or working outside the home. The number of zeros on the paycheck is also irrelevant. It has to do with the heart of a man and how he was created by God. The same is to be said for a woman. While men can be compassionate, women are generally noted as being more compassionate than men. Men are adventuresome, while women are nurturing. We all know men can nurture and some women like adventures, but the point is that men are created one way and women another. When we attempt to fit both men and women into the same mold, we have lost our understanding of the image of God.

Men and women are equal and yet different, and both are created in the image of God. If you only look at the man to see the image of God, you will only see part of the image. The same is true if you only look at the woman. However, when you see man and woman together, you begin to see the fuller picture of the image of God. Together they reveal what God is truly like; strong and courageous, tender and compassionate, rugged and dignified, while being nurturing and humble; hard, soft, bold, and shy; the list could be endless, but the truth is revealed. When a man and a woman are together, the image is seen more fully than if they are apart.

Human Beings Were Created To Live In Fellowship With One Another And With God

The image of God, which is present in both man and woman, extends beyond the character of the two as individuals to the relationship God intended us to dwell in together with each other and with Him. The relationship of the Persons of the Trinity is one that is based on intimacy and love, not on authority and structure. As has been stated previously, the Father does not exercise authority over the Son and Spirit, but He dwells in eternal relationship with them, expressing

His love for them. The Son and the Spirit are not subservient to the Father, but they dwell in His love and seek to accomplish not simply His will, but what will bring joy to His heart. This relationship is one of mutual submission out of love and the desire to express love to one another. What is seen in God was intended by Him to exist in our relationships with one another. This was intended to be true for the relationships between all people, but it is to be most clearly seen as a man and woman dwell together as husband and wife.

When a man and woman come together in marriage, God has a desire to work in and through them to reveal His image in a fuller way than can be seen anywhere else in all creation. Each of us, as human beings, lives our lives in many different relationships. We begin as a son or daughter, possibly a brother or sister. We fill the role of nephew or niece, grandchild, boyfriend or girlfriend, best friend, etc. We will have many acquaintances and relationships throughout life, but none is like marriage. While we live in relationships with many different people, we are never joined to another person in the same way as we are to the one we marry. Marriage is unique in all creation because in marriage, and marriage alone, two people are made one. This is one of the greatest miracles of God, which, though visible every day, is overlooked by most people in our world. The truth is that though we may be parents, and the fulfillment of this role enables us to grow in our understanding of the Father's love for each of us as His children, we are not even one with our children. Marriage, the union of a man and woman, is unlike any other relationship in the world, for this relationship was created by God for a man and a woman to exist in fellowship with one another, even as God does in Himself.

When the understanding of the various roles of man and woman are skewed, the result is devastating to what God originally intended. If the husband assumes the role of having total authority and insists his wife is subservient to him, the result is that a woman loses her true identity and her real value as a child of God created in His image. In this type of relationship, the desire of God to reveal His image in and through the couple is thwarted. The same end result becomes a reality when a woman is disrespectful to her husband, and in this way, she rejects his role in her life as the one chosen by God to be the source of security and protection for her heart. When a couple is constantly battling for control in the relationship, the image of God is lost. If we desire to be blessed by God and live in relationship with each other as a man and woman in such a way that others may see in us the image of God, then we must step back and rethink our understanding of marriage and the roles of husband and wife.

So many people approach marriage as a contractual agreement, a fifty-fifty relationship. When this view is taken, the result is predetermined – there will be problems. For example, what happens if this 50/50 contract is not adhered to completely? If the husband fails to give his fifty percent, the wife is no longer obligated to give her fifty percent, if she even had a desire to do so. Thus, begins the downward spiral into conflict. We expect others to uphold their end of the bargain, and we are upset when they fail to do so. This is not the image of God that is to be revealed in our lives individually or as a couple. If this is the relationship in which a couple lives, what is it revealing to others concerning our relationship with God? If God dwelt with us in a contractual agreement in which each person was responsible for his or her obligations, where would we be? God is committed to His part, and we, in turn, are to uphold our end of the bargain.

But what happens when we fail to follow through with our responsibilities? God is no longer obligated to uphold His promises because we have failed on our part. There are those people who have approached their relationship with God based on this flawed human model, and the Biblically true answer is that God is faithful even when we fail in our obligations because of His grace. While this sounds good, and it is true that grace does prevail, it is still approaching our relationship with God from the perspective of the Law and not the Gospel. God does not place a burden of responsibility upon us as His children. Grace means that God has done it all for us, and there is nothing left for us to do but receive the gift which is freely given.

Do the members of the Trinity dwell in a conditional or contractual relationship with one another? The answer is no! They dwell in a relationship based on unconditional love for each other. This is the relationship God desires to reveal to us and to reveal through us to the world. If we attempt to define the relationship of God as He dwells in eternal love, each member of the Trinity, then we must use a complete number. God the Father is one hundred percent committed and in love with the Son. There is no limit to His love, and He places no conditions on it. The same is to be said for the love of the Son toward the Father, as well as the love of the Spirit for the Father and Son, and from them to Him. Each dwells fully and completely in love with one another. It is their love for each other that moves them to do what brings joy to the heart of the other.

Actions are not taken to ensure love but rather to express love. Thus, we can truly say that Jesus came into this world to be Savior not only because of His love for us but because of His love for the Father and His desire to do what pleased the Father's heart. This said, He also loved us and died to be our Savior and, in so doing, brought joy to the Father's heart by bringing His lost children home to Him. This understanding of being one hundred percent lovingly committed to the other is what God desires to reveal to the world in and through our relationships with each other, especially in the relationship of husband and wife.

The husband who is reflecting the image of God loves his wife fully and places no expectations on her in order to ensure his love. He loves her 100% even if she is unable on a given day to return 100% of her love to him. The desire is the same as God's desire, to give, not receive. God loves us and is one hundred percent committed to us. He loves us without any conditions or expectations in order to be loved by Him. For example, when Jesus was hanging, bleeding, and dying on the cross, how many people were loving Him? What was He receiving? Nothing, zero! He was dying for the sins of the world while, at that moment, receiving nothing except judgment. His desire was to give love without any conditions, only to love. Having loved us completely, He now receives all love freely given to Him in return. In the relationship of a couple, the wife should be on the receiving end of the husband's love. He is to give one hundred percent of who he is to love her with no conditions or expectations for a return. Only in this way is he truly reflecting the image of God in his life. The wife, having received full and complete love from her husband, is moved to love in return, not because she must, but because she wants to. I have yet to hear a woman say that if her husband was one hundred percent committed to her and in love with her, she would not be happy. When you are loved, your response is to love in return. If the husband gives one hundred percent with no expectations, then anything he receives in return from his wife is a gift. This is grace and gospel lived out in our lives with each other. Turn the image upside down and have a wife who gives one hundred percent to her husband with no expectations. The husband is blessed and naturally desires to love in return, and all the wife receives is a gift. In this, the image of God and the love shared among the members of the Trinity is realized in our lives and lived out for the world to see.

Understanding what God's love for us is truly like enables us to live in a secure relationship with Him, and it frees us to love one another in the way God created us to love. There is no greater sadness in the heart of a pastor or any other Christian than to hear someone say that they "hope" they will go to heaven when they die. God does not want His children to live in fear of the future. Scripture is full of the promises God has made to each of us, and because He never fails to keep a promise, we can live secure in the knowledge we have a future home for eternity. It is only when we misunderstand God's love and grace that we live in insecurity. If God truly loves us with a one hundred percent committed love, then we do not have to worry about the future and what He desires for each of us. He has revealed in both word and deed what the desire of His heart truly is. He sent Jesus to die so that we might be restored to a relationship with Him in which we can truly know how special and loved we are by Him.

The opposite is to approach God as if His love for us was conditional. When this is the case, a person is forever wondering if God is angry or upset with him or her and this person dwells in insecurity. This doubt about the future has led many people to simply give up on God. He is too harsh a taskmaster. He is distant and uncaring. His demands for perfection are too high, and we can never meet them, so why try? It is sad to hear those who are resolved to going to hell because they are confused about God's love. There is a problem; it is called sin. But the confusion lies in the understanding of life here in this world and the promise of salvation in the world to come.

CHAPTER NINE

FELLOWSHIP WITH GOD

"Those who walk with God, always reach their destination."

– Henry Ford

In the garden, God came walking (Genesis 3:10). He came to live in relationship, actually deeper than that, in true fellowship, with Adam and Eve. The verse says they hid from God because they were naked. For the first time, there was fear and shame in the heart of the man and the woman. Fear because they had sinned against their God. Shame because they were no longer worthy to stand in His presence. What was the big deal? What was so special about the tree? Why did it matter so much? It is sometimes humorous to hear people speak of the apple or to say "I don't think it was an apple because I like apples. Maybe it was a persimmon tree." It was not the character of the fruit, but the tree which was unique. Not the tree itself but what the tree represented.

Place yourself in God's position or that of Adam and Eve. God gave all creation to Adam. Nothing in all creation was outside of his reach. He was given authority over all creation which is exhibited in the fact he was charged with naming all creation. Like a parent naming a child, no one else has that right. All was his except the one tree; this God kept for Himself. From God's perspective, why place the tree in the garden to give temptation to the man and woman? The answer is not that difficult. How are your people to worship You and live in relationship with you as their God if everything is under their authority and nothing belongs to You? It was the tree that enabled the man and woman to live in a relationship with God by which they understood He was God, and they were His children. God had given them everything else, all creation. The one tree He kept for Himself, and by this one tree, He enabled them to live knowing He was their God. He was above and over them to bless them. They lived in humility before their God by honoring Him in regard to the one tree. When they took of the tree, they sought to elevate themselves over God and live without Him. This was Satan's temptation that they would be like God. What they did was take from God the only symbol of His dominion in all creation. Thus, the relationship with God was broken, and the result was fear and shame.

On that day, man ran from God, and he has been running ever since. But notice, man ran away from God, but God ran to man. God came with questions, beginning with *"Adam, where are you?"* God was calling to Adam. He was searching for him, wanting him to return to the relationship which existed before the fall. It has been said that the entire story of the Bible, from the fall in the garden to the end, is a story of God searching for His children. Did God know the man and woman had sinned before He came into the garden? The obvious answer is yes!

God did not have to come into the garden to discover man's sin. He could have simply sent angels to drive them out of the garden. The angels could have delivered the same message to them. God came personally; why? Because He loved His children. He was searching for them, yearning for them to return. He came, and they ran. He called, and they fearfully answered. Instead of being honest and accepting the responsibility for what they had done, each attempted to shift the blame to the other. This, no doubt, broke the heart of God because, in this shifting of blame, the fear of God is seen. Fear in the sense of being afraid of God. What was God to do? Sin had become a reality, and the result was a world that would now suffer the consequences of sin until the end of time. The consequences were real, but just as real is the promise God gave to His children on that day, a promise exhibited in word and deed.

In their shame, Adam and Eve hid from God because they were naked. Their nakedness, which was before the fall natural and beautiful, was now to be hidden as something which was shameful. Their attempt to hide their nakedness is an apt symbol of the futility of man's attempts to deal with sin. The two sewed fig leaves together to make coverings for themselves. What is going to happen in a day or two? The fig leaves will dry, turn brown and break apart, revealing their nakedness. So, it is with all man's attempts to deal with sin. We make every attempt, but in the end, all efforts fall away, and we are left standing in our sin, unable to hide our shame. This is not what God desired for Adam and Eve, and it is not what He desires for us today.

The Promise Is Given With A Visible Act Of God

On that day, God made a promise. The promise was spoken as judgment to Satan, but it is a promise for God's children. The Seed of the woman will crush the head of the serpent. The destroyer will be destroyed. What was lost will be restored. The very first Gospel promise was given within moments of the man and woman standing before God as sinful human beings. God did not berate them or humiliate them because of their sin; He immediately gave them hope in the form of the promise of a Savior. Then before sending them out of the garden to face life in the world, God acted in a visible show of grace for them. Moses writes that God made coverings of animal skins for Adam and Eve. Before this day, there had never been death in the garden. One of the consequences of the fall into sin was to be death, both spiritual and physical death for the man and woman. But Adam and Eve had never seen death before. Until this moment, death was an abstract concept. But here in the garden, God killed! God shed blood! God acted in grace to cover the nakedness of their sin. God shed first blood to address sin, all its consequences, and shame. Imagine, if you will, Adam and Eve standing over the body of the animal(s) God killed for them. Imagine the overwhelming emotions they must have felt as they realized the innocent one died that they might live. Here is the grace of God in "deed" for them. A visible illustration for them to understand. The shedding of the blood of the one who is innocent will cover their sin. God promised a Savior would come, and in this act, He revealed the sacrifice this Savior would make.

Jesus Is The Action Of God For Us

Jesus is described as the *"Lamb of God who takes away the sin of the world"* (John 1:29). I have often wondered if the animal(s) killed by God in the garden was a lamb. The thing about a lamb is that it is totally defenseless. A lamb has no claws to slash or teeth to bite. The role of the shepherd described by David is one of loving and protecting the sheep from all harm and danger because they are unable to protect themselves. Jesus came as an innocent one and as a defenseless one to become the sacrifice for the sins of all mankind. But His decision to be our Savior was not an afterthought. God knows all things, and He knew, even before creation, that Adam and Eve would sin, and His creation would be lost to sin and Satan. Before the first words of creation were ever spoken, God knew He would lose us all. So why did He create? Why not let creation be a passing thought and spare Himself all the heartache and pain?

The answer is love. Even before creation, when the idea of humanity existed only in the heart of God, He loved us. His love for us was not just an emotion born of an idea. It was a real, true, everlasting love that moved Him to make choices and decisions which would cost Him dearly. It has been said that creation itself was the very first act of grace. God created all of us, knowing even as He spoke those first words that He would have to die for us to have us as His children. Knowing all this, He spoke, "Let there be light," and creation came into being.

The love of God for all humanity began before the creation of the world and has its origins in the heart of God and in the heart of our Savior. There is a significant passage of Scripture that is often used of God's people choosing faithfulness and service to God found in Isaiah chapter six, *"Who will go for us and whom shall I send . . . Here am I send me."* It has often been used by pastors to answer the call to serve God in the ministry. While this is certainly an appropriate application of this passage, it goes much deeper! The key is found in the understanding of the Hebrew language. There are different words used for God throughout the Old Testament. This is often identified in the English translations of the Bible by how the word "Lord" is printed. When it is seen in all capital letters, LORD, the Hebrew word is "Yahweh." Yahweh is the proper name for God as He revealed Himself in the Old Testament.

When Moses stood before the burning bush and asked God His name so He could tell the Children of Israel who had sent him to deliver them, God answered Yahweh. It is a name that identifies all three persons of the Trinity and, in some contexts, only the Father. There is another word that is used, "Adoni." This word is translated in the English Bible as "Lord" with lowercase letters. This word, Adoni, is never used of the trinity or of the Father, but only when addressing the Son of God prior to His incarnation. In Isaiah six, *"the LORD," Yahweh, said to "my Lord," Adoni, whom shall I send? God the Father is speaking to God the Son, and it is the Son who says, "Here am I, send Me."*

Before the words of creation were ever spoken, Jesus was already willing to become our Savior. He was accepting the sacrifice He would make in order to love us and bring us back to the Father, even before He called us into existence. The reason for this willingness is truly His love for us, even before we were created, but it is more than this. Jesus was moved to become our Savior because of His love for the Father. He loves the Father's heart, and as His Son, He desires to do all which is pleasing to the Father, not out of obedience, but out of the desire to fully and completely love His Father. To do what He did simply as an obedient Son means that His sacrifice is motivated by obligation or the Law! To do what He did for the Father out of a motivation of love means His willingness was that of Gospel! Everything points to the Father and His heart. Our lives lived in relation to God today are still about the Father's heart. Jesus came to be the sacrifice for our sins so we could be restored as children of our Father. The Holy Spirit is present in this world to work faith in our hearts so we can believe in Jesus as our Savior and be restored to the Father! Everything is about each of us, knowing we have a Father in heaven who loves us and would stop at nothing to have us with Him forever.

In becoming Savior, Jesus was loving the Father and also loving each of us. His sacrifice on the cross accomplished what the heart of the Father desired: the forgiveness of sins. The barrier which separated each of us from God has been destroyed, and we can now live in the security of knowing God loves us and wants to walk with us here in this life until we walk with Him in the life to come. Having said this, it is easy to move quickly to our life in Christ without fully realizing the magnitude of the sacrifice Jesus made for each of us. The cross was much more than nails and blood. The reality of sin, shame, and judgment were present, and unless we understand what happened on Calvary, we will miss the depth of God's love for us.

When the Apostle Paul writes to the Corinthian Christians, he says, *"For our sake He made Him to be sin who knew no sin, so that in Him we might become the righteousness of God"* (2 Corinthians 5:21). In this one powerful passage, Paul states what Jesus did for us on the cross, what He actually endured. Many people hear of Jesus bearing our sins upon the cross as if He simply put them on like a coat to see what they felt like for a while. The truth goes much deeper, to the very fiber of His being. Paul says Jesus was made to be sin for us. This means that when Jesus took our sins to Himself as He was upon the cross, He took our sins and made them His own. I want you to understand what this means to the fullest degree! Have you ever told a lie?

Almost everyone would have to admit that at some point in their life, they have told a lie. Have you ever been caught in a lie? Again, most would say "yes." What did it feel like? Do you remember the shame and humiliation of being caught in a lie and the consequences of a broken relationship and the punishment you endured because of it? When Jesus hung upon the cross, He took your lie and made it His own. He became the liar, and as such, He felt the shame of being a liar, and He suffered the broken relationship which just one sin caused, and He took the punishment that one sin deserved so you could be forgiven of that one sin! Now, extrapolate that one sin out to include all the sins of all people throughout all of human history. It will make your stomach turn and your heart ache. Jesus became a murderer, thief, child molester, rapist, liar, adulterer, pedophile, and abuser; the list is endless, for the sins of mankind are endless. He did this not just once but for each and every sin of each and every person who has or who will ever walk on this earth. Having taken the sin, He also felt the guilt and shame of what He had become. As One who was guilty of sin, He was punished for the sin.

It is impossible for any of us to understand what it means that Jesus took an eternity of hell and judgment upon Himself during the six hours He was on the cross. It is not for us to understand how it happened but to know and believe that it did happen for us. The sin was real, the guilt was present, the shame was overwhelming, the judgment was dispensed, and the fellowship was broken. His cry from the cross, *"My God, My God, why have You forsaken Me,"* is the cry of aloneness. There had always been unity in the Trinity. The Father, Son, and Spirit living in a perfect relationship of love. Never could One look to the Other and not see and experience love personified, except on this day. For the first and only time in eternity, the Son looked to the Father, and the Father turned away. The devastation was overwhelming. The Father, Who is holy and Who cannot look upon sin, turned away from the Son as He hung upon the cross, having become guilty of our sin, all sin. He was an unworthy sinner, and as such, He was judged. Jesus died alone and abandoned by God the Father, but He died with the assurance and hope of the Father's love. He yielded His spirit to the Father and bowed His head, and died.

The Father accepted the Sacrifice of the Son, the resurrection declares this to be true, and it is in this hope that we live.

CHAPTER TEN

THE HEART OF GOD YEARNS FOR HIS CHILDREN

"It is staggering that God should love sinners; yet it is true. God loves creatures who have become unlovely and (one would have thought) unlovable. There was nothing whatever in the objects of his love to call it forth; nothing in us could attract or prompt it. Love among persons is awakened by something in the beloved, but the love of God is free, spontaneous, and unevoked."

—J. I. Packer

Through the sacrifice of Jesus upon the cross, sin has been paid for completely, and we are restored and have become who God the Father always desired for us to be, His children. It is tragic that so many people believe God is a distant and uncaring God, Who is always looking for us to make a mistake so He will have an excuse to punish us. This is not the heart of the Father. His desire is to bless, not to curse. His desire is to shower His love upon us. He is not looking for a reason to withhold it. We are who we are by the grace of God! And who are we? We are children of our heavenly Father, sinners who have been forgiven by the blood Jesus shed upon the cross for us. We did not deserve it, and we certainly did not earn it, yet it was given to us freely because God loves us. This is what we call grace! So why is it that so many Christians live their lives seeking to win approval from God? We are bombarded with untold messages from society that declare to us that we need to take hold of our own destiny. We need to pull ourselves up by our own bootstraps. If we don't work hard and make the sacrifices necessary, we will never succeed. Every message the world proclaims is that you must accomplish for yourself what you desire. This may work in the world, but it has no place in our relationship with God. The very moment we believe anything we do affects the Father's attitude toward us, we have lost Jesus and His cross!

Imagine, if you will, a child with his/her parent. What is the life of that child like? Is the relationship one which is based on the actions of the child? What if, in a family, a child does something good, the parent responds with words of affirmation and declares love for the child. If, on the other hand, the child does something which is displeasing to the parent, the pronouncement is made, "I can't believe you did that. I can't stand you. Get away from me. I don't love you anymore!" Once the child does something to make amends for the mistake, the parent once more declares love and acceptance for the child. What would life be like if this scenario were to be repeated for every action of the child? The yo-yo of acceptance and rejection in the relationship would be constant in the child's life, and it would make that child's life unbearable. If we saw this type of action from a parent toward a child, we would openly declare that it was wrong and that the person was a bad parent. Yet, we turn around and live as if this is exactly how God the Father relates to us! One minute we do something good, and He smiles at us, and the next minute He is frowning on us because we made a mistake. If this is true, then God the Father is a bad parent, and He doesn't understand how to love His children.

Thankfully, this is not the heart of our Father! He loves us with an everlasting and unchanging love. It is the desire of the Father to have each of us dwell with Him forever. The Scriptures are clear on this great truth. Passages such as John 3:16 speak of the Father's love as well as great truths like Matthew 25:41, where Jesus states that hell is a place *"prepared for the devil and his angels."* Hell was not created for people! It is not, nor has it ever been, the desire of the Father to send anyone to hell. It is true that people do go to hell, but this grieves the Father's heart. It is not what He wanted. He sent Jesus precisely so we would never have to face judgment and could live assured of an eternal home with Him. What each of us needs to fully grasp and incorporate into the depths of our hearts is that "what you do does not define who you are." So, who are you? If you understand that Jesus bore your sins upon the cross and suffered the judgment you deserved, and you believe in Him and the promise of God that you are forgiven, then you are His child.

As a child of the Father, you can live with the assurance that He loves you no matter what you do. Understand, we can do things and make choices that are displeasing to Him, and many of our choices in this life do have consequences, in this life. But our actions here do not change or nullify the love the Father has for us. You are who you are by the grace of God, and this will not change. When you do what is pleasing to God, it does not make Him love you more, and if you do what is displeasing to Him, He does not love you any less. His love for you is absolutely unchanging!

What can be said of those who believe in Jesus as their Savior can also be said of those who don't. God loves all people equally; as Paul told Timothy, *"This is good, and it is pleasing in the sight of God our Savior, who desires all people to be saved and to come to the knowledge of the truth,"* (1 Timothy 2:3-4). The heart of God loves all people equally. Jesus came and died for all people, those who believe in Him and those who have rejected His love and His sacrifice for them. It is not about what we do! Those who do not believe in Jesus earn no favor with God when they do good and no animosity from God when they do evil. The only difference between a believer and an unbeliever is faith. Faith in the sacrifice Jesus made for everyone gives assurance to the one who believes, whereas the one who has no faith has no assurance.

It Can Be Difficult For Us To Believe In God's Limitless Love

You are a child of God! This is the reality of your life if you believe in Jesus. This is a reality that is not based on anything you do or don't do, be it good or bad. It is a reality based on the heart of the Father who loves you and has promised to walk with you here in this life and bless you to dwell in His presence for all eternity. The challenge is that often we find it difficult to accept this free gift of forgiveness from God, and we carry great guilt in our lives, which in turn makes us believe we are unlovable by God.

God created us as emotional beings! This is another great aspect of the image of God which we bear for the world to see. God does have emotions. He expresses joy, and He expresses sadness. He gets angry at sin and, at the same time, has compassion for the sinner. Emotions are real and an extremely powerful force in our lives, a force that has the ability to affect not only each of us individually but those around us. When Adam and Eve sinned against God, they were filled with guilt, and it was this guilt that moved them to run and hide from God. Many people today, those within the church and those not connected to a church, are running and hiding from God. Their guilt over past mistakes or even current situations moves them to believe they are unworthy to be a child of God, and so they run. Some run to choices that enable them to escape the pain they feel in their hearts. Drugs and alcohol abuse are often just a symptom of what is truly happening in the heart of a person. Others move from one relationship to another, seeking solace but never finding the solace for which they seek. There are those who work rather than sleep; others shop until the store employees know them by name. There are as many different methods of escape as there are people running. One truth remains the same, the harder and faster we run away from God, the more earnestly He is running to us.

There are those who base every decision in life on what they feel at any moment in time. The problem with this is that often what we feel is the opposite of the truth. I feel unworthy, so God must hate me. We have already seen this is not true. Just because we do not feel something does not mean it is not true. There are many people who struggle with love and acceptance in their lives. Often this is something to which they have been conditioned from childhood. A distant or harsh parent will raise a child who always questions if anyone can truly love them. When that person becomes a Christian, he/she may often doubt that God truly loves them. There are those who will even say, *"I know God loves me because He promised He would.*

I am going to heaven, but I will enter the back door and sit in the back row. God doesn't really want me, but He has to take me because of His promise."

Even in God's love, there is the uncertainty of worth or value for people who think this way. Have you ever been close to a parent who has a newborn child? There is pride and excitement which overcomes bashfulness and a willingness to share the good news even with complete strangers. We have all heard of the new father who is handing out cigars to complete strangers in celebration. How many new fathers will insist that every visitor must go to the hospital nursery window to see his new baby, and we all know that his baby is by far the most beautiful and most special child in the nursery, in fact, in the entire world. Does our heavenly Father love us less than an earthly father loves his child? Instead of running from God, listen to His heart and the joy He has over you. When He turns His eyes upon you, there is a stirring in His heart, a smile on His face, and a joy that cannot be contained. All the heavens rejoice as God proclaims His undying love for you. He picks you up and wraps His arms around you, and you dwell securely in the love of your Father. You are the one who captivates the heart of your Father, and He is filled with a father's pride that you are His child.

You may not feel like all this is true. You may feel unworthy and unaccepted, and because of this, you have been running and hiding most, if not all, of your life. It is time to stop running and let God love you as He desires to. Do you want to understand the excitement God has in His heart for you? The Old Testament prophet Zephaniah states something which has been overlooked by most Christians. He says, *"The LORD your God is in your midst, a mighty one who will save; he will rejoice over you with gladness; he will quiet you by his love; he will exult over you with loud singing"* (Zeph. 3:17). Can you imagine the God of eternity lifting His voice and singing because He is excited to have you as His child? Well, imagine it, because it is true!

This is the reality of who you are as one who was created by God to be the object of His love. Because He created you for this purpose, you cannot escape it. It is true whether you feel it or not, if you believe it or not, or even if you simply don't understand it. Truth is truth, and it cannot be changed, and the truth is that you are loved by God. What you feel and what you do will not change God's heart for you. It is a reality that finds its origins in the heart of God, which was present before the world was created and which will exist when creation is folded up and put aside like an old garment. God loves you not because of anything you have done but because of who you are! You are His child, born of His love to be blessed by Him forever.

CHAPTER ELEVEN

WHAT THE CHURCH ON EARTH SHOULD BE

"The Church lies at the very center of the eternal purpose of God. It is not a divine afterthought."

— John Stott

The fact that we are the children of God is a reality that is undeniable and unchangeable, based upon the grace of God in Christ. The challenge we face first is understanding this, and secondly, living with this reality in our everyday lives. Unfortunately, most Christians who are connected to some type of church or congregation seldom hear of this reality in the Sunday morning services they attend. Even more unfortunate are those Christians who have attended churches where they have been hurt because they were all too human and, as a result, have forsaken any sort of church life and who now face the struggles of life in this world without the love and support of fellow Christians.

There are a few who are willing to teach the truth in such a way as to dare to shock people with the hard realities of God's Word and who are willing to suffer the consequence of doing so for the sake of the Gospel. For example, when was the last time you heard a preacher speak on the topic of sin being fun? In truth, sin is fun! If it were not fun, we would not be so eager to do it, whatever sin it is. It is fun to drink and have a good time with your friends, especially when you are underage. Drugs cause powerful feelings in a person's body. And we all know the pleasures of sex and the addictions which can be formed when what God created is taken outside of the context of marriage. From the money gained from illegal business deals and the pleasure gained from what this money can purchase to the lies we tell to gain power and prestige over others, we choose to engage in these and all sinful activities because we receive some gain or pleasure from it. We can see this simple truth in the garden of Eden when Adam and Eve were tempted. The fruit was pleasing to the eyes, good for food, and desirable to make one wise, is how Moses wrote it. There was a pleasure and personal gain to be obtained by disobeying God and eating of the Tree. Do you think they would have been so eager to eat the fruit if it looked gross and smelled of rotten eggs? The truth is sin is fun!

If we are honest with ourselves and others, we will admit this and then deal with the reality of temptation and sin in an open and honest way. When we simply speak of how horrible sin is and how wretched a person is who engages in a particular sin, we have missed the mark of addressing sin in an honest way. Yet, what is the attitude which exists in most churches today? There are those sins which are taboo and those sins which are acceptable and even thrive in the midst of church life. Taboo sins are those which are counted as so undeniably present in a person's life that the person trapped in the sin is no longer counted as worthy of being a member of the church or at least a member in good standing. In almost every church, divorce is one sin that results in a man or woman being abandoned and even shunned by those who were once called friends. Abuse is another sin that cuts both ways. The abuser is an immediate outcast, and the victim, if he or she is honest, is quickly moved to the fringe of relationships because no one is willing to deal with the hurt and pain involved. This results in the victim being victimized all over again! For the man or woman who struggles with feelings for a same-sex relationship, there are two choices, churches that condemn the person and say they are going to hell, do not pass go, do not collect your two hundred dollars.

The other choice is to connect with a church that has set aside God's Word and which condones relationships that are contrary to His will in the lives of His people. What does the Gospel of grace tell us? How are we to treat each and every person in this world? The Gospel of grace would declare an individual sinful person as one who is loved by God and cherished by Him. This same Gospel would also speak to the sin which has enslaved a child of God. It is not the calling of any person in this world, Christian or not, to condemn another person who is loved by God. We need to relearn what it means to condemn sin while at the same time loving the person who is trapped in the sin. The goal and mission of the Church is to reveal the love of God in Christ in such a bold and impactful way that the person who has been entrapped in sin is captivated by the love of God. Only then will such a person come to know Christ as Savior, and with the indwelling and power of the Holy Spirit, this person will then be able to overcome the hold which sin has in their life and be set free.

All these sins, and a host more, give rise to the acceptable sins which are alive and well in the churches of today. Pride, judgementalism, and self-righteousness are present in almost all, if not all, churches of today. We seem to have come to a point in the church today where we can discern by a person's life what is present in their heart. With this understanding, we are ready and willing to save God the time and effort of waiting until judgment day; we judge the person! Oh, how far we have fallen! How many times have we stood in the hallway of a church and heard a "concern" someone has about another member of the church? We share prayer concerns only as a means to share with others all the "dirt" we have collected on someone. Any way you cut it, this is gossip wrapped in sanctimonious talk. There is also the idea that those who have been in a church for a number of years carry more weight than a newer member. A new idea or a new way of doing something is an immediate strike against this new member, and they are often made to feel that they should keep their ideas to themselves. The phrase "We have never done it that way" is in some churches a mantra to unchanging traditions, and God help the one who dares to change anything.

What is devastating to a person's spiritual life and which no doubt grieves the heart of God is when a person is truly struggling with sin, and no one really cares. While it is true that sin is fun, the consequences which result from our choices can destroy lives and relationships. Sin leaves all of us suffering. We are hurting on the inside, filled with guilt and pain, and many times abandoned by those we believed would help and support us. The sad reality is that when a person begins to suffer the consequences of sin, that person will often turn to the church for help and support. What does the church do? Many times, once the sin is known to the members, the individual is looked down upon and made to feel like a second-class member. Like the big red letter "A" upon the chest, the person is marked for the sin they committed and will forever wear this label. This, of course, is never spoken openly but understood by those who look down their noses at the person. These, who are so quick to label, are the same who believe they are just a touch better than others; after all, they attend every service, give their offering faithfully, and serve in the church with great fervor. God must certainly be more pleased with them, right?

The catchphrase which has made its way from billboards to bracelets is the letters WWJD, or What Would Jesus Do? Certainly, a good method for discerning what course of action to take when contemplating a decision. But if this is all we understand this phrase to mean, we have fallen woefully short of our understanding of Jesus' desire to bless and guide our lives. What Would Jesus Do should first direct the attitude of our hearts long before it directs the actions of our hands. What would Jesus do if He encountered a person who was trapped in sin? Any sin? What was His attitude toward sinful human beings? Fortunately for us who are God's people today, we do not have to wonder. We have the attitude of Jesus' heart revealed in Scripture if we are but willing to look and see what His heart is truly like.

How We Should Minister To One Another

One day Jesus was asked to make a pronouncement based on the Law of Moses. A woman was caught in adultery (John 8). She was caught in the "very act," is what the text says. That means they drug the woman out of her adulterous bed but failed to bring the man along as well. She was placed before the men of the city. She was openly humiliated and declared worthy of being stoned to death. This was the perfect opportunity for the Pharisees to trap Jesus. There was no denying this woman was a sinner, so what would He do? If He upheld the Law, she would be stoned. If He excused her sin, He was breaking the Law. They believed they finally had a way to use His words against Him and thus prove Him to be a false teacher. What Would Jesus Do? The self-righteous stood with stones in hand. The woman was cowering, half naked and scared. What Did Jesus Do? He spoke a word that caused the men gathered to turn their eyes away from the woman and onto their own hearts. *"Let the one who has no sin cast the first stone (vs. 7)."* The Scripture says that one by one, they dropped their stones and departed, beginning with the oldest who were gathered. The older men were more discerning than the younger and had lived long enough to understand that they could not judge others when the light of self-righteousness was cast upon them so bluntly. When all had departed, and Jesus knelt by the cowering woman, He spoke to her, *"Woman, where are they? Has no one condemned you?"* She said, *"No one, Lord."* And Jesus said, *"Neither do I condemn you; go, and from now on sin no more"* (John 8:10-11). There was no self-righteous attitude toward her. Was she guilty of sin? Yes! Jesus, as the holy Son of God, could have judged her, but He didn't. She was guilty, but He was gracious. *"Neither do I condemn you"* are some of the sweetest words in all of Scripture. Words spoken to a sinner who was undeniably guilty. Words spoken to give peace to the heart and hope for eternity. The heart of the Father and thus the heart of the Son does not want to condemn but to bless and save.

If we look, we can see a consistent pattern throughout the Gospels of how Jesus actually dealt with people. Simply put, He dealt with people in one of two ways. The self-righteous received from Him unyielding condemnation and judgment. Few statements in the entire Bible are as harsh as those directed toward the Pharisees by Jesus. Matthew, who had been a tax collector, recorded many such words spoken by Jesus. These words probably brought great comfort to Matthew because, as a former tax collector, he had been on the receiving end of the self-righteous pronouncements made by the Pharisees.

Matthew records seven "woes" in chapter 23 of his Gospel. In each of the pronouncements made, Jesus blasts the Pharisees for their self-righteous attitude toward others. In each of these passages, Jesus addresses a different aspect of the Pharisee's abuse of the people of God.

> *"But woe to you, scribes and Pharisees, hypocrites! For you shut the kingdom of heaven in people's faces. For you neither enter yourselves nor allow those who would enter to go in. Woe to you, scribes and Pharisees, hypocrites! For you travel across sea and land to make a single proselyte, and when he becomes a proselyte, you make him twice as much a child of hell as yourselves.*
>
> *"Woe to you, blind guides, who say, 'If anyone swears by the temple, it is nothing, but if anyone swears by the gold of the temple, he is bound by his oath.' You blind fools! For which is greater, the gold or the temple that has made the gold sacred? And you say, 'If anyone swears by the altar, it is nothing, but if anyone swears by the gift that is on the altar, he is bound by his oath.' You blind men! For which is greater, the gift or the altar that makes the gift sacred? So whoever swears by the altar swears by it and by everything on it. And whoever swears by the temple swears by it and by him who dwells in it. And whoever swears by heaven swears by the throne of God and by him who sits upon it.*
>
> *"Woe to you, scribes and Pharisees, hypocrites! For you tithe mint and dill and cumin, and have neglected the weightier matters of the law: justice and mercy and faithfulness. These you ought to have done, without neglecting the others. You blind guides, straining out a gnat and swallowing a camel!*

> "Woe to you, scribes and Pharisees, hypocrites! For you clean the outside of the cup and the plate, but inside they are full of greed and self-indulgence. You blind Pharisee! First clean the inside of the cup and the plate, that the outside also may be clean.
>
> "Woe to you, scribes and Pharisees, hypocrites! For you are like whitewashed tombs, which outwardly appear beautiful, but within are full of dead people's bones and all uncleanness. So you also outwardly appear righteous to others, but within you are full of hypocrisy and lawlessness.
>
> "Woe to you, scribes and Pharisees, hypocrites! For you build the tombs of the prophets and decorate the monuments of the righteous, saying, 'If we had lived in the days of our fathers, we would not have taken part with them in shedding the blood of the prophets.' Thus you witness against yourselves that you are sons of those who murdered the prophets. Fill up, then, the measure of your fathers. You serpents, you brood of vipers, how are you to escape being sentenced to hell? Therefore I send you prophets and wise men and scribes, some of whom you will kill and crucify, and some you will flog in your synagogues and persecute from town to town, so that on you may come all the righteous blood shed on earth, from the blood of innocent Abel to the blood of Zechariah the son of Barachiah, whom you murdered between the sanctuary and the altar.

As you read over the previous verses, it is shocking how direct and pointed Jesus is when dealing with the Pharisees. He did not cut them any slack. The reason for this is that they were the spiritual leaders of the people, and as He says, through their legalism and self-righteousness, they were shutting the kingdom of heaven to the people of God.

The Two Ways Of Jesus

Jesus had two ways of dealing with people. He had little tolerance when confronted with the self-righteous religious leaders of the day. Just as true was the fact that when Jesus came in contact with individuals who were broken by sin, He would accept them where they were at in their sin and love them. He would assure them that God is a loving God Who desires to forgive. Having done this, He would encourage them to live their lives differently than they had previously. Examine the previous example of the woman caught in adultery. The woman was guilty beyond all doubt, yet Jesus went to her and accepted her for who she was without any condemnation. He then assured her of His forgiveness with the words, *"Neither do I condemn you."* Having assured her of His forgiveness, Jesus then encouraged her to make different choices in the future, *"Go, and from now on sin no more"* (John 8:11). We certainly need to understand Jesus is not expecting her to live a perfect life from this point forward, but rather that the sin in which she had been engaged was to no longer be a part of her life. Knowing this sin is forgiven in such a pointed and complete way by Jesus would have enabled her to face future struggles with sin, having the hope and assurance of God's acceptance and forgiveness.

What is seen in Jesus' actions and attitude toward this woman is revealed in His relationships with countless others throughout His ministry. When you examine the texts of His encounters with Zacchaeus, who was a tax collector, Peter, who denied Him, the woman at the well, the Centurion, the man born blind, and all others who were broken by their sin, you see the same attitude, the same heart of Jesus. Because of this, we are able to have hope in our lives today as we struggle with the reality of our own sinfulness and the consequences which bring pain and guilt into our lives. We are no different than Adam and Eve. When we sin and the consequences become evident, our first instinct is to run and hide from God. This can include withdrawing from church life and relationships with other Christians. A person can become so ashamed that he or she will feel unworthy to even walk into a church, believing God no longer wants them as His child. What was God's action toward Adam and Eve? He came to them, and He loved them even in their sin. He promised deliverance through a Savior to come, and He provided for them what was needed as they faced life in a fallen world. When we sin, God does not turn away from us. The opposite is true; we turn away from God. Our guilt and shame cause us to run! But what does God do? He comes to us. He comes in love and grace and calls to us, even as He called to Adam. Not in an audible voice, but He calls in the words of the Gospel. He calls, desiring to give us forgiveness and restore us to a right relationship with Himself.

It has been said in the past that God made it simple, His people complicated it. The promise given to Abraham was that through Him, all the nations of the world would be blessed. What did Abraham's descendants do? They took the truth of God's Word and hoarded it to themselves and not only refused to share it with others but judged others as unworthy of God's love. When Solomon built the temple, it was to be a place where all the nations of the world would stream to the Lord our God. Later generations set up a hierarchical system by which certain people could draw closer to God than others. There was the court of the Gentiles, a place for proselytes (non-Jews who worshiped the God of Israel), women had their own section, Jewish men could go a little closer, and the priests could enter yet closer. Why did Jesus fashion a whip out of rope and drive out those who were selling and trading at the temple? They had set up for business in the court of the Gentiles. The bleating of sheep and the bellowing of cattle, along with the arguing over the exchange rate for temple currency, would have made it impossible for the gentiles to worship God. The people of God made it impossible for anyone except those just like them to approach God. The temple is gone, the sacrifices are ended, and we don't have a marketplace in the church, but we have set up new obstacles which make it almost impossible for anyone who is not just like us to approach God.

In some churches, there are unwritten standards. We have grown accustomed to the fact that there are churches that expect a person to dress a certain way and others who say jeans are ok. We have coffee bars to appeal to a specific group and other churches that are extremely traditional and even turn a suspicious eye to those less formal. We have churches that are focused on a specific ministry theme, such as outreach to college students, ministry to the elderly, motorcycle ministry, and even a "cowboy" church that seems to quickly make the transition to a building and a structured form for church. There are denominational churches and non-denominational churches, churches with traditional music and those with contemporary music. We have taken the idea of marketing the church to a whole new level, and in all the business of "church," we have left Jesus out of the equation. God made it simple, His people make it complicated.

What Is God's Desire For His People?

What is it God desires for the Church in the world? Are we to be so rigid that we are un-accepting of anyone who believes differently? Or are we to be so careless that a person is left to believe anything they want, regardless of what Scripture says? Are we to minister to only specific groups or seek to include everyone? Now, there's a thought! Why not minister to everyone equally, regardless of who the person is, where they are from, or even the color of their skin. Can a church today actually do this? The answer is yes if a church is ready and willing to seek the heart of the Father and learn to relate to people with the same love He has for them. We have to ask ourselves, "What does the Father desire?" Everything in the Scriptures point to one great truth, the Father desires to share His love, His heart, with us. It does not matter what a person has done or will do. It certainly does not matter what a person's ethnic background is, their economic status, or even their attitude toward other Christians or God Himself.

There is nothing about a person which would move God to cease to love them or abandon them. If we, who are the Church in the world today, are going to truly minister to people, then we must have this same heart for all people. When a person makes a mistake or outright sins, our attitude should be to run toward the person, not away from them. This is what God has been doing since the beginning of time. Only when we begin to understand this will we begin to become the people, the Church God yearns for us to be. We will make mistakes, and we will blow it at times, and therein is the grace of God for each of us. When we sin, we live in the confidence that God's heart for us has not changed. He loves us for who we are and not for what we do. We are His children, and we will be forever! This is the heart of our Father.

CHAPTER TWELVE

GOD KNOWS ALL ABOUT YOU AND HE STILL LOVES YOU AND WANTS YOU

"I have given God countless reasons not to love me. None of them has been strong enough to change Him."

– Paul Washer

If we truly are the children of God and it is in His heart to love us and reveal Himself to us, then in what way are we to live, and how is this understanding to make a difference in our lives as His children? It has been stated previously that God desires to walk with us. He came into the garden to walk with Adam and Eve. His desire today is the same desire which filled His heart in the garden. It is in the heart of God the Father to bless His children, and one of the greatest blessings is for each of us to live with the assurance of knowing God loves us and wants us as His own. Jesus told the parable of the Pearl of Great Price. The merchant went and sold all he had to obtain that one pearl. It was prized above all else in his life. When God looks at you, what value does He place on you?

Each one of us has, at times, believed that others are more important to God than we are. There will always be those individuals who seem to be more committed, more involved, or even more sanctified than we are. It is easy to begin to believe that God loves them in a greater way than He loves us. This could not be further from the truth. When God was in eternity, before the creation of the world, when He peered into the future and looked upon the face of each and every human being who would ever walk upon this earth, He saw you. He looked upon your face, stared into your eyes, and loved you. He loved you with His whole heart, and because He loved you, He committed Himself to you as His most prized possession. You are His child, and He loves you as only He can, with a Father's love. He made the choice to create this world as a place to reveal Himself, His love for you. What you need to understand is that if everyone in all human history had remained perfect, if Adam and Eve had never sinned and all their children had remained faithful to God except for you, if you were the one, the only one who had ever sinned and as a result had been separated from God, Jesus would have come into this world to die for you.

When Jesus went to the cross, He was loving His Father and accomplishing the desire which filled His Father's heart. He was bringing you back to the One who loves you above all else. At the same time, Jesus was loving you; He was taking your sin and guilt upon Himself because He did not want you to carry that burden any longer. He wants you to be free to celebrate who you are as a child of God, which is impossible if you are struggling under the weight of your sin. Jesus took your sin and guilt upon Himself, shedding His blood so you can live today knowing you are completely forgiven. If sin is forgiven and guilt is taken away, then there is no shame or unworthiness to stand in the way of your relationship with God. So many people live with the belief that God is completely disappointed with them. So many are ashamed to even turn their faces toward heaven, believing themselves to be unworthy. When you think about God sitting upon His throne and looking at you, how does it make you feel? Are you scared? Do you want to run and hide?

That is how Adam felt, and that is what Adam did! He ran from God and tried to hide. How did that work out for him? God entered the garden and sought him out. Adam could not hide from God any more than you can hide from God. Just because you ignore Him doesn't mean He is ignoring you. What is God doing right now as He turns His face toward you? Do you believe He is frowning? Is He disgusted with you? Will He only look for a moment and turn away? None of this is true! God is looking at you right now, even as you are reading this, and because of who you are as His child, He is loving you, and He is smiling upon you. Yes, that's right, God is smiling as He looks at you. You can be sure of this because you are the desire of His heart, and He loves you. You are the source of joy for His heart. He is fully and completely accepting and forgiving of you, and His desire is for you to live your life differently than you have in the past. He wants you to stop being scared of Him and live each day knowing you are loved by Him, and He desires for you to live with the assurance of His blessings here and now, as well as for all eternity.

The reality of God loving us and smiling upon us should have an immense impact on our lives. So much time has been lost to either running from God or seeking a way to appease His wrath through the things we do. What we need to remember, and in fact, remind ourselves of every day, is that we are not the ones who established this relationship. Our sin separated us from God, and there was nothing we could do to change our situation. Our feeble attempts to please

God and overcome the reality of our sins are laughable. We are helpless in our sins, but we are not without help. We could not go to God, so God came to us, just like He came walking in the Garden to find Adam. He came in the person of His Son, and He still comes today with the word of promise and hope. He comes to walk with us in this life until the day comes that we walk with Him in eternity. Knowing that eternity is secure and safe in the hands of our Father enables us to face the challenges of today without having to worry about tomorrow. What is the promise almost everyone has heard? *"I will never leave you or forsake you."* If we have the absolute promise spoken personally from Jesus that He will never leave us and never forsake us, what is there in this life we cannot face and ultimately overcome? He is present with us to bless us even as we struggle through the challenges we face. He is here to support and strengthen us so that we know that regardless of how dark it looks or how overwhelming it feels, these things will pass, and brighter days are in our future.

CHAPTER THIRTEEN

OUR FUTURE LIFE WITH GOD – A VISION OF IMAGINATION

"Once a man is united to God, how could he not live forever?"

– C.S. Lewis

In the modern age of medical technology, there are numerous accounts of individuals who have died but who have been resuscitated and live with the memory of a bright light and a feeling of overwhelming joy. What these experiences may very well reveal is the fulfillment of the promise Jesus made to His disciples and all who believed in Him. In the Gospel of John, the account is given of Jesus teaching about the end of each of our lives in this world. He states that He is going to prepare a place for us and that He will return to receive us to Himself, and we will dwell with Him forever (John 14). The promise given is assured through the resurrection of Jesus from the dead. His resurrected life enables our eternal life.

The question we seek to understand, and which is not as clearly discerned in scripture, is "What happens in the transition from life in this world to life in the next?" From what we can discern from the passages of the Bible which address our eternal life is that in an instant, that exact moment when life in the body ceases, the spirit of a person who has been bound to the body is set free. Freed from the confines of the body, which is fallen from its original, intended state, the spirit is able to enter into a full relationship with God in which a person abides in His presence. At that moment, we will fully know even as we have been fully known by God. A person is freed from the sinful nature which has made it impossible for him to know God fully, His presence, or His will for his life. In that instant, we stand in the presence of God, the Father, Son, and Holy Spirit, and it will be revealed to us how much we have been loved by God from eternity.

The question which often arises from most who discuss the topic of heaven is the confusion over what heaven will truly be like. There are those who have an image of heaven as simply floating on clouds, while others have been led to believe it will be like an eternal church service that will never end, neither of which gives a true description of what eternity will be like. There are multiple images given in Scripture of eternity; a return to the Garden of Eden, living in mansions, and walking on streets of gold. We are not given exactly what heaven will look like. What is revealed in the Bible is that heaven is so far beyond our comprehension that the most wonderful images possible in this world are used to give us a glimpse of its grandeur. More importantly than what heaven will be like in a physical sense is what it will be like for all who are present in a spiritual sense.

To Fully Know And To Be Fully Known

Have you ever walked down the street or through the mall and observed people? You say "hello" to a stranger on the street, usually out of some sense of being kind, but you don't know that person. Enter the mall of your community the day after Thanksgiving and count the people you actually know. For most of us, the number would be quite small. We live in the midst of strangers, and even among the people we do know and have a relationship with, there are barriers to knowing them fully and intimately. In Matthew's Gospel, the following account is given.

> *"And he was transfigured before them, and his face shone like the sun, and his clothes became white as light. And behold, there appeared to them Moses and Elijah, talking with him. And Peter said to Jesus, "Lord, it is good that we are here. If you wish, I will make three tents here, one for you and one for Moses and one for Elijah."* (Matthew 17:2-4)

Moses had led the children of Israel to freedom from slavery, and Elijah had been used by God to call the people of God to repentance. These were two of the greatest leaders of the Old Testament people of God. It has often been said that these two were present at the transfiguration of Jesus because He is the fulfillment of what these two represent, the Law and the Prophets. However, the question which is important for our understanding is this, "How did Peter, James, and John know these two individuals were Moses and Elijah?" There were no photographs or drawings which depicted who these individuals were so that they might have recognized them. There are no descriptions that have been handed down through history. These were two complete strangers who had appeared with Jesus, yet the apostles knew who they were. How? The only possible answer is that standing in the presence of the glory of God, knowledge was given to them, which was beyond what they could naturally have in this world.

What would it be like to walk through the mall at Christmas time and know every single person? To truly know them! Not just a person's name, but to truly know the person, their personality, their heart. What would it be like to have an intimate relationship based on true love and to have this relationship with every person you would see? Because God fully knows each of us and because we will not only be fully known but know fully, we will share an intimate relationship with our God and with each other. It sounds impossible to us on this side of heaven. We can barely keep the stories straight for the few people we do live in close relationships with here in this life. The idea of intimately knowing millions and millions of individual people seems impossible to us. Yet, when we realize that sin and all the consequences of sin are taken away and that we are freed from the limitations which now inhibit us, we can begin to understand that what God has in store for us is far greater than we can ever fully comprehend in this life. But understanding this is only part of the story. There is so much more we will experience beyond living in an intimate relationship with God and with each other.

One of the favorite pastimes in our culture is living vicariously through other individuals. Hollywood exists for this very reason. Some of the favorite Friday night activities for most people in our society revolve around the movie theater, DVDs, and television. We identify with the stories we watch, and we become emotionally connected to the characters. There are romantic love stories that draw us into an intimate desire to be connected with another human being in such a deep way. There are bold adventures that embolden our hearts to aspire to greater things. There are tragedies that grieve our hearts and move us to tears. There are even times when we wish beyond hope that such a story could be the story of our very lives. We often leave the movie theater, returning to our mundane existence, and are left yearning for more in this life than what we have. It is this yearning for a great story that captivates our hearts and our attention. There are very few people who are bored when they enter a movie theater and even fewer who actually will choose to leave a movie part way through. In truth, we get drawn up into the story, and in some ways, we wish it would never end.

Glorifying God In Eternity

With this said, what will it be like to sit at the feet of Moses and hear him recount all which God did in his life personally and through him to bless so many people? Since Moses will fully know each and every detail of what actually happened and how God was working in every life and every heart, he will be able to tell of God's salvation, painting vivid pictures with absolute clarity. What was it like to stand before the burning bush? What did it look like, feel like, smell like? Oh, how his heart trembled when he returned to Egypt as God directed, to stand before Pharaoh, an individual he had grown up knowing.

He will tell of standing before Pharaoh, declaring God's pronouncement to *"Let my people go,"* while explaining why God hardened his heart and the purpose it served to bless the children of Israel. He will recount the singing and celebration when the plagues ended, and the people walked into freedom, and how their singing turned to cries of despair when Egypt's armies stood ready to destroy them. Did the people actually see the fish, even whales, swimming alongside them in the wall of water as they passed through the Red Sea? What did it sound like for the waters to come crashing down on the Egyptians who chased them into the sea? And what did manna taste like?

We will sit and listen with understanding as Moses recounts all which God did to save His people. His tale will captivate our hearts because it has all the elements which move us and draw us up into something greater than ourselves. There is adventure, terror, and tragedy. The story is one of romance and love coupled with absolute devotion and self-sacrifice. There is even the element of betrayal and the grief of the heart betrayed. In all this, we will listen and see through the eyes of Moses all God did until they stood on the verge of entering into the Promise Land. When Moses has finished his tale, he will turn his attention to God, who is listening, sitting upon His throne, and Moses will bow in humble adoration before His God, our God, who did all this because He loves us. All of heaven will resound with the praise of God for His love and faithfulness. We will declare His glory for the salvation of His people. Then there will come a point when Joshua steps forth and picks up the story where Moses left off. Crossing the Jordan, the battle of Jericho, the conquest of the land. Battle by battle, blow by blow, we will hear of all God did to fulfill His promises to His people and make it possible for each of us to stand in His presence.

This scene will be carried out by each and every one of the saints of God. From David when he stood before Goliath, to Solomon who will speak of the day the temple was dedicated and God was present in His glory. We will hear of the glory of God from the lips of Isaiah, Daniel, Jeremiah, Miriam, Hannah, Elizabeth, Caleb, Abraham, Isaac, and the list will go on and on. What will it be like for Mary to speak of the angel's visit or of Joseph telling of what it was like to father the Son of God? At the end of each account, all of heaven will turn attention to

God upon His throne, and bowing in humble adoration, the praise of God will fill eternity and resound through heaven.

Then will come the moment when all the saints of God will turn their attention to you. You will rise, and with great joy and excitement, you will begin to speak. The story you tell will be with absolute clarity for you will know fully all God did in you, for you, and through you for His glory. From the moment of your conception to the instant you saw His face when you entered eternity, you will know all He did for you. Every moment He was at work to save you. From the working of the Spirit to bring you to faith to every turn you made that saved your life. Every stop light which seemed such an inconvenience, but which saved you from an accident to the casual word spoken by you which changed someone's life by opening the door for God to bless them. In the same way, you were captivated by the stories of Moses and Elijah, all of heaven will listen as you retell all God did in your life. Most of us believe our lives are boring and meaningless, but at that moment, what we share will be no less dramatic than the stories of Peter and Paul. These great saints will listen attentively as you proclaim with absolute clarity God's working in your life, and when you have told your tale, what will happen? All of heaven will bow before the throne of God and lift their voices on high to sing the praises of God for His faithfulness to you. They will praise Him for how He worked in your life and through you to bless others. All of heaven will celebrate how God made the very day of your salvation possible, and the celebration will last for all eternity.

EPILOGUE

"When one has once fully entered the realm of love, the world — no matter how imperfect — becomes rich and beautiful, it consists solely of opportunities for love."

— Søren Kierkegaard

To you, my reader, my brother or my sister, fellow saint in the household of God, thank you. I have written this book so that together we can begin to see our God as He truly is. Because the world has become so used to viewing God in perverted ways, many people hear someone speak of God and immediately close the ears of their hearts. God is not Who most people think He is. He is a Father, or as Brennen Manning reveals in his book <u>The Ragamuffin Gospel</u>, God is Abba or Daddy. I am deeply indebted to my family, especially my wife, who has loved me like no other. She was the first one I told of my abuse as a child. She was the first to show me, unconditional love. Her love for me opened the way for me to truly be able to understand the love of God, our Father's heart. I share this with you because sometimes we need a tangible, real-life example of unconditional love. Steph did this for me, and over the years, I have changed from a person who believed in God to a man who knows God. I do know Him because He has chosen me to be one of His sons! I couldn't say that at one point in my life. God was distant and unreachable to me. My guilt and shame created a wall, a barrier between my heart and His. It was not on God's part I assure you.

Looking back, I can clearly see how my Father was there. He loved me even when I was running away from Him, and He pursued me. He would not let me go. Patiently over time, love won out. With living examples of love and the heart-wrenching experience of dealing with my past, I found myself standing before God with empty hands and an empty heart. There was nowhere else to go. No more running, no more hiding, no more living behind the wall I had erected. The wall came tumbling down as I realized that there was nothing I had ever experienced and nothing I had ever done which has changed my Father's limitless love for me. I have felt His embrace. I have experienced the soulful tears of healing in my heart, and I know today that I am loved by God.

Please never underestimate not only your Father's love for you but how He wants to use you to tear down the wall separating Him from His children. So many people are living today where I used to live. Believing in God, even that He is a God of love, but they are too damaged, too broken to be wanted by Him. Your tangible expression of unwavering limitless love for them may very well be God working to chip away at the wall and open the way for true love, the love of the Father's heart, to win.

Know I will be praying for you. I may not know your name, but as my Father and I talk, there are times when I just ask Him to soften the hearts of those who don't understand. Those whose lives and circumstances have caused them to run so far away from Him. Often it is the things that are done to us, events out of our control which create the most guilt and shame in a person's life. When any good father sees his child hurting, the instinct is to draw close and take his child in his arms and comfort them with his assuring love. In this, an earthly father is revealing the Father's heart. He is the One who seeks to draw close to us when we are hurting, Who takes us in His arms and assures us of His love. A love that will never waver or lessen, but a love which is true and, if we can think it possible, growing for all eternity.

May you, my fellow brothers and sisters walk our journey of faith with the assurance of our Father's love. Our Father's Heart truly is set on us. And just so you know, if my imagination is correct, I can't wait to hear your story.

www.ingramcontent.com/pod-product-compliance
Lightning Source LLC
Chambersburg PA
CBHW022133080426
42734CB00006B/344